CREATIVE STRATEGIES

to TRANSFORM SCHOOL CULTURE

CREATIVE STRATEGIES

STRATEGIES

to TRANSFORM SCHOOL CULTURE

JOHN F. ELLER • SHEILA ELLER

A JOINT PUBLICATION

CORWIN
A SAGE Company

NATIONAL ASSOCIATION
OF SECONDARY SCHOOL
PRINCIPALS
promoting excellence in middle and high school leadership

For information:

Corwin
A SAGE Company
2455 Teller Road
Thousand Oaks, California 91320
(800) 233-9936
Fax: (800) 417-2466
www.corwinpress.com

SAGE Ltd.
1 Oliver's Yard
55 City Road
London EC1Y 1SP
United Kingdom

SAGE India Pvt. Ltd.
B 1/I 1 Mohan Cooperative
   Industrial Area
Mathura Road, New Delhi 110 044
India

SAGE Asia-Pacific Pte. Ltd.
33 Pekin Street #02-01
Far East Square
Singapore 048763

Printed in the United States of America.

Library of Congress Cataloging-in-Publication Data

Eller, John, 1957-
Creative strategies to transform school culture / John F. Eller and Sheila Eller.
      p. cm.
Includes bibliographical references and index.
ISBN 978-1-4129-6117-2 (cloth : alk. paper)
ISBN 978-1-4129-6118-9 (pbk. : alk. paper)

   1. School management and organization—United States. 2. School environment—United States. I. Eller, Sheila. II. Title.

LB2805.E45 2009
371.2′07—dc22   2009005579

This book is printed on acid-free paper.

09 10 11 12 13   10 9 8 7 6 5 4 3 2 1

Acquisitions Editor:	Hudson Perigo
Editorial Assistant:	Lesley K. Blake
Production Editor:	Cassandra Margaret Seibel
Copy Editor:	Cate Huisman
Typesetter:	C&M Digitals (P) Ltd.
Proofreader:	Charlotte J. Waisner
Indexer:	Jean Casalegno
Cover Designer:	Michael Dubowe
Graphic Designer:	Karine Hovsepian

Contents

Preface

Schools today are under pressure to increase student achievement, meet the needs of all students, solve the problems of society, and remain fiscally responsible. Sounds like a pretty simple mission, right? It's an understatement to say that working in a school has become increasingly complex and stressful. One result of this increased stress in many schools has been a gradual deterioration of the work environment or climate. With the emphasis on increasing academic performance, some schools have forgotten about the emotional issues of their teachers and students.

This book has been designed to help principals as they begin to think about and make plans to improve the climate and ultimately the culture of their schools. In designing this book, we have relied on several information sources. First, we examined research related to the importance of a positive climate and culture in relation to student achievement. Researchers are in agreement that a positive school climate and culture, in which there are high expectations for students, is one of the key ingredients of student success. We also used information we have gathered over the years from our work with principals, and we include here some of the strategies they have found to be helpful in improving the climate and culture of their schools. Finally, we have used our own experiences in helping to turn around school cultures. Together, we have almost 30 years of experience as school principals. In most of the schools we have worked in, we have been able to improve the working and learning conditions of both staff members and students through our ability to improve both the climate and culture of each school. We share this experience with you in this book.

One of the aspects of this topic that can be confusing for principals is identifying the difference between school *climate* and school *culture*. We offer some researchers' perspectives on this question in Chapter 1, but we want to offer our perspective here as well.

In general, the climate of a school refers to the feel or tone of the school. The climate is really based on how the school feels from day to day. Since the climate is somewhat variable, it can be influenced by interventions somewhat rapidly. For example, if a school principal perceives that staff meetings are dull and boring and decides to use music as a way to make meetings more energized, the impact is almost immediate. The climate of the meetings will be improved.

School culture, on the other hand, is more stable or grounded than climate. Since the culture is more stable or ingrained than the climate, it may take several long-term and consistent interventions to make a shift in the culture. Relative to the smaller effort that a principal may put forth to improve faculty meetings as discussed in the previous example, he or she may have to use music in staff meetings consistently over a long period of time, and couple that with participation activities and other strategies, in order to begin to change the school's culture around meetings. To improve the culture related to meeting participation may take a year or longer of consistent and focused intervention. When the new meeting behavior becomes an internal part of how the staff perceives and operates its meetings, a change in culture has occurred.

This book is designed to fill a specific niche: improving the climate and culture related to the *adults* in the school. We have found that working with the teachers and other staff members is an important place to start with school climate and culture efforts. Once the staff members are on track, efforts with the students can begin. Student climate and culture interventions are not discussed in this book, even though many of the strategies presented are likely to trickle down to the students once they have been used with staff.

Since we understand the difficulties in changing culture, we wanted to provide this book as a guide for others who are attempting to change their school cultures. The book has been designed to be practical rather than theoretical in nature. We did provide some of the background and theory in the first two chapters so you can understand the context we are coming from in looking at the concepts of climate and culture. The bulk of the book contains practical, proven activities and strategies that will work to improve the climate and culture of a school. We have provided a wide variety of ideas for you to consider. All of these activities and strategies will work in schools, but you need to select the ones that you are most comfortable with and that you think will work best for your school. In the end, keep moving forward to make your school all it can be.

Good luck as you work to improve the climate and culture of your school—it is a journey worth taking!

John and Sheila Eller

Acknowledgments

Corwin gratefully acknowledges the following reviewers:

Boyd Dressler
Associate Adjunct Professor
Montana State University
Bozeman, MT

Stephen D. Shepperd
Principal
Sunnyside Elementary School
Kellogg, ID

Leslie A. Standerfer, EdD
Principal
Estrella Foothills High School
Goodyear, AZ

Darryl L. Williams
Principal
Montgomery Blair High School
Silver Spring, MD

About the Authors

John F. Eller has had a variety of experiences in working with adults over the years he has been in education. His experiences include working with educational leaders at Virginia Tech University; developing teacher leaders in a master's program; serving as the executive director of the Minnesota Association for Supervision and Curriculum Development (ASCD); working as a principal's training center director, being an assistant superintendent for curriculum, learning, and staff development; and serving as a school principal in a variety of settings. In addition to the work he does in training and supporting facilitators, John also does work in the areas of dealing with difficult people; building professional learning communities; employee evaluation; conferencing skills; coaching skills; strategic planning strategies; school improvement planning and implementation; differentiated instruction; leadership for differentiation; employee recruitment, selection, and induction; supervisory skills; and effective teaching strategies.

He has a doctoral degree in educational leadership and policy studies from Loyola University–Chicago and a master's degree in educational leadership from the University of Nebraska–Omaha. John's writing includes a volume on substitute teaching, *The Principals' Guide to Custodial Supervision, The Training Video Series for the Professional School Bus Driver*, and articles for *Superintendents Only*. In addition, he has authored or coauthored several books published by Corwin: *Effective Group Facilitation in Education: How to Energize Meetings and Manage Difficult Groups, So Now You're the Superintendent!*, and the best-selling *Energizing Staff Meetings*.

Sheila Eller has worked in a multitude of educational settings during her career. Currently a middle school principal in the Moundsview (Minnesota) School District, she has also served as a principal in other schools in Minnesota and Illinois, as a university professor, as a special education teacher, as a Title I math teacher, and as a self-contained classroom teacher in grades 1 through 4. Sheila is also a member of the executive board of Minnesota ASCD and has been a regional president of the Minnesota Association of Elementary School Principals. She has done advanced coursework in educational administration and supervision at St. Cloud State

University, and she has a master's degree from Creighton University in Omaha, Nebraska, and a bachelor's degree from Iowa State University.

Sheila is a regular presenter at ASCD national conventions, sharing her expertise on the topic of effective staff meetings and multiage instruction. While she served as a professor at National-Louis University in Evanston, Illinois, she worked on the development team for a classroom mathematics series that was adopted by several districts in the region. Her classroom and instructional techniques were featured on a video that was produced as a complement to this series. She works with educators in developing energized staff meetings, school improvement initiatives, multiage teaching strategies, employee supervision, and other teaching and learning content areas. In addition to coauthoring this book, Sheila has coauthored the best-selling *Energizing Staff Meetings*.

1

Culture and Climate

Joan was offered a job as the principal of Riverton High School. She was told by the assistant superintendent that this school was one of the hardest schools in the district. The staff had a reputation of running principals off, being rude to each other in meetings, and not getting along as a staff. When new teachers started working at the school, they were told to sit back, do their jobs, and be quiet. The climate of the school was negative, and over time, the negative climate helped to make the culture of the school negative as well. Joan was facing a true challenge as the principal of this school.

She started the year by taking the time to meet each staff member and get his or her unique perspective on the school. During the first staff meeting, Joan addressed what she had learned from the staff interviews, and her ideas to help people at the building learn to work together. In her initial staff meeting, Joan helped the staff set expectations for her and each other. These expectations would be used to help set the school climate and begin to impact the culture of the school. At each staff meeting, she had a brief activity planned to help the staff learn more about each other. When disagreements came up between faculty members, Joan acted as a mediator. If a staff member got out of line, Joan met with the person and addressed the issue.

Throughout the year, Joan worked hard to hold herself and the staff to the expectations set during that first meeting. For the first time in years, there was clarity in staff expectations, and issues were taken care of right away and not allowed to fester and get worse. Joan had begun to make the climate be more welcoming and positive, and she was beginning to have an impact on the culture of the school as well. Her work was far from done, but she was beginning to make progress in changing the school.

Joan faced a situation not uncommon in schools today. As a result of many factors, some schools have become unpleasant places to work. Many principals are looking for ways to improve both the climate and the culture of their schools in order to improve opportunities for student learning to occur. Joan was beginning to be successful in her quest to improve the school; others are not so fortunate. What makes the difference between success and failure for principals facing schools in which the climate and culture are negative?

ABOUT THIS CHAPTER

Climate and culture are two factors that principals need to work on as they improve their schools. As you read the chapter, pay attention to the following points:

- The difference and the relationship between climate and culture
- Subcomponents of climate and culture
- The importance of these two elements in improving schools

SCHOOL CLIMATE VERSUS CULTURE

These aspects of schools get mixed together and can cause some confusion for school leaders. We provide brief information outlining the differences between the two in Figure 1.1. We will go into more depth on each later in the chapter.

School Climate

Since a school's climate refers to its day-to-day operations, it is more malleable than a school's culture, and we will start our discussion of creative strategies with an introduction to school climate. Many researchers offer definitions of school climate. Hoy and Hoy (2009) offer the following definition for school climate:

> Organizational climate is a general concept that refers to the teachers' perceptions of the school's work environment; it is affected by the formal organization, informal organization, and politics, all of which, including climate, affect the motivations and behavior of teachers. (p. 329)

This work environment aspect of climate works well for those of us in leadership positions. Climate becomes the feel and atmosphere of a

| Figure 1.1 | School Climate Versus Culture |

School Climate	School Culture
The climate of a school is the immediate feel or tone that is felt or experienced on a day-to-day basis. Climate is a subset of culture and works to build toward the school culture. School climate can be immediately impacted because of its moment-to-moment nature.	The culture of a school is the deep foundation or base that governs many other aspects of the school's operation. The culture of a school is stable and consistent over time. Changing the culture can be somewhat difficult like changing the course of a large ship moving in a certain direction.
Positive Climate Examples	Positive Culture Examples
<ul><li>At the front entrance of the building, student work is displayed and highlighted.</li><li>A volunteer greeter welcomes people to the building.</li><li>Teacher-to-teacher and principal-to-teacher interactions are positive and illustrate personal regard.</li><li>The principal respects the instructional expertise of teachers and provides positive and constructive feedback.</li><li>Teachers interact outside of the workplace; these relationships benefit the workplace and the students.</li></ul>	<ul><li>When new teachers are hired, veteran teachers take it upon themselves to connect and make them feel welcome and supported.</li><li>When new teachers are hired, veteran teachers take it upon themselves to connect and make them feel welcome and supported.</li><li>The staff utilizes a formal process to pass on information about students at the end of the year to the teachers in the next grade level or content area; the focus is on providing a positive "hand-off" to the next group receiving the students.</li><li>The "hero teachers," or the staff members that the rest of the staff idolizes, are those that have gone the extra mile to support student success.</li><li>Teachers understand that the principal observes their classes to help understand what is happening and to provide guidance rather than to look for problems.</li><li>Staff meetings are organized around collaboration and problem-solving; informational items are handled through newsletters and e-mail.</li></ul>

(Continued)

(Continued)

	• Teachers support creativity and individuality in student work; this is evidenced by their reinforcing all student attempts and posting a variety of work in their classrooms and halls.
Negative Climate Examples	Negative Culture Examples
• As people enter the building, they are greeted by a list of rules and regulations. • Staff members pass each other in the halls without saying "hello." • Staff members do not eat together; individuals work alone. • Principal-to-teacher and teacher-to-teacher interactions are artificial and lack a sense of relationship and personal regard. • Teachers talk about others behind their backs; issues related to personal expectations are not addressed. • The school halls are dull and dark; paper and other litter are seen in and outside of the school. • The school is dark and dreary.	• Teachers work to rule (stand up and leave meetings right when their contract day is finished, do the minimum work required by the district, etc.). • Negative or outspoken staff members who cause trouble are idolized. • The lounge or work area is always inhabited by negative people who talk negatively about students; any positive talk is quickly squelched. • The principal is known for pointing out only mistakes in teaching during feedback conferences; teachers have great anxiety related to evaluation observations. • Teachers report that their opinions and ideas are not listened to or used in improving the school. • People work only within their specific role or job assignment; no help or assistance is provided to colleagues. • New teachers are left on their own to prove themselves; if they don't make it, staff members are not concerned. • People work with their doors closed and do not share ideas or strategies.

school. Many people comment that they can "feel" the climate of a school right when they walk in the building. This "feel" permeates through the building from the front office to the classrooms. The good feeling we experience as visitors also helps the school to be a comfortable and safe place for students to grow and learn. Educational leadership expert Dr. John Hoyle of Texas A & M offers the following observations:

> School climate may be one of the most important ingredients of a successful instructional program in a district or school. A broad term, "climate" refers to the environment of a school as perceived by its students, staff, and patrons. It is the school's "personality." (1982, p. 6)

The environment or personality of the school does describe its climate. It is important to think about this personality as you begin to understand the climate of your building. See how the climate of a school is illustrated in the following example:

Philip, the principal of Lang Middle School, believes in operating a school that has a positive climate. He works hard to make people feel welcome when they enter the building. He has asked his custodial staff to make sure the front entrance is always clean and bright. They sweep the halls in the front of the building at least four times each day. Philip has also had them install more lighting in the front entrance so that it is bright and cheery. A rotating exhibit of student work is displayed in the front entrance so that visitors can see the bright and colorful examples of student work when they enter the school.

Office staff members cheerfully greet visitors, asking how they can help them. Even though the front entrance to the building is also a security area, the office staff overcomes the security feeling through their friendly actions. New visitors to the school are asked to sign in, given a colorful visitor's badge to wear, and then are escorted to their destination by a parent volunteer or student ambassador. These volunteers point out positive aspects of the school as they escort visitors to their destinations. This positive attitude rubs off on the students and parent volunteers, who take great pride in their school and tell others about its positive climate. People continuously comment that Lang Middle School has a positive school climate and is a good place for students and teachers.

Philip's story is simple but powerful. Are there problems and issues at Lang Middle School? There are several issues the staff is working together to address, but the first impression that people have when they enter the school is that things are under control and organized. The school seems to be a safe place for learning and a place the people like to be. This initial impression of a school is an important aspect of school climate. If the building is welcoming, people attending school, working in, and visiting the building have a good feeling about being there. If the initial impression is negative or even neutral, people's impression and attitude can be shaped toward the negative. Let's look at another school and see how different its climate is compared to that of Lang Middle School:

> At Oakview Middle School, visitors enter the building and are greeted by an empty hallway. The floors are swept once daily, and a few papers are scattered about. Once visitors enter, there is a sign directing them to go to the main office (which is to the left about 20 feet from the main entrance). When visitors reach the main office, they see a large counter. Behind the counter, office staff members are answering the phone, writing passes for students, and processing paperwork. Normally visitors are not greeted right away but must wait a few minutes before someone notices them and asks if he or she can help them. Many times, because they are busy with other chores, the office staff members have to tell visitors that they will be with them in a minute.
>
> Once the visitors have identified their destinations, they are given directions to get there and issued a pass. Nobody accompanies visitors to their final destinations. Many parents comment that they feel unwelcome at the school and limit their visits as much as possible. Students of the school do not take pride in the building, and there tend to be paper and other items on the floors.

Oakview may be the most nurturing school in the community, but the overall impression that visitors get is negative. The school will have to work hard to overcome this feeling with students, staff, and visitors.

These two schools present different first impressions and ultimately have set up different climates for learning. Even though the schools presented here have seemingly slight differences in the appearance of their front entrances, the climates of these schools are vastly different. The feel or tone of each school is set within the first 20 feet of the entrance. The climate is positive at Lang and a little less than positive at Oakview.

The previous examples are simple but powerful and illustrate that purposeful efforts do pay off in a more positive climate. Simple and straightforward strategies to improve school climate compose one focus area of this book. Throughout the various sections and chapters of the book, we will be sharing simple ideas that you can use to immediately improve your school climate.

The climate or personality of a school is one key to the success of the students and the adults in the learning environment. Climate tends to be the moment-to moment aspects of the school personality. These moment-to-moment aspects do tend to work together to begin to define a more pervasive aspect of the school—the organizational culture. In the next section we will briefly examine the aspect of school culture.

School Culture

School culture is related to climate but more comprehensive (and pervasive) than climate. The culture is the result of the combined climate issues that have been in place and reinforced over an extended period of time. Let's take a look at the experiences of Cathy, the principal of Dorsey Elementary School, in relation to the aspect of school culture:

Cathy, the principal of Dorsey Elementary School, works hard to ensure that the staff members contribute to the positive culture of the school. She understands that since culture is a long-term and pervasive aspect of a school, it needs constant maintenance. One aspect of Dorsey's culture that is strong is related to the problem-solving process. For years, staff members have been engaged in providing insights and input into helping to solve problems at Dorsey. This was a new aspect to Cathy when she came to the school, so she spent her first year there learning how the process worked and seeing how it fit her operating preferences as a principal. Cathy was able to work with the staff to identify the types of decisions or problems they wanted to be involved with and used this information to develop a decision-making matrix. This matrix is used now to determine the level of involvement the staff needs or desires related to solving problems. Cathy is able to quickly determine when to involve the staff and when to move forward on her own using this matrix. The staff is also happy that she understands their preferences and uses them to help focus their involvement. The culture of the school (the desire of the staff members to be involved in significant decisions) has been honored, while Cathy is able to move forward independently on issues that are less significant to the staff.

In this example, it's easy to see that the staff members at Dorsey Elementary School believe in participating in decisions. Teachers like to be involved in solving problems and making decisions, and this desire is ingrained in the long-term behavior of the teachers. The desire to be involved in decisions is a part of the *culture* of the school. School culture relates to long-term and embedded beliefs, behaviors, and attitudes that impact the core or foundation of a school. Several authors provide insight into the concept of organizational culture.

Edgar Schein, one of the pioneering authors in the area of organizational culture, provides insights into the aspect of culture. In his book, *Organizational Culture and Leadership* (2004), Schein provides the following thoughts:

The culture of a group . . . can be defined as a pattern of shared basic assumptions that the group learned as it solved its problems of external adaptation and internal integration, that has worked well enough to be considered valid and therefore, to be taught to new members as the correct way to perceive, think, and feel in relation to those problems. (p. 17)

Other authors offer their perceptions of school culture: Sergiovanni (2007) writes, "Culture is generally thought of as the normative glue that holds a particular school together" (p. 145). According to Hoy and Hoy (2009), "It's useful to think of organizational culture as a pattern of shared orientations that bind the organization together and give it a distinctive identity" (p. 319). Taking these definitions into account, we find that the concept of culture refers to the deeper, more foundational aspects of the school's operation.

Schein provides a listing of the most common attributes that are shared by groups of people that make up the culture of an organization.[1] As you review this list, think about the kinds of behaviors you see that exemplify these components:

1. Observed behavioral regularities when people interact (the language they use, the rituals in place, etc.)

2. Group norms (the implicit standards and values that evolve)

3. Espoused values (the articulated and public principles and values the group appears to be seeking to achieve)

4. Formal philosophy (the broad policies that guide the group's actions toward stakeholders)

5. Rules of the game (the implicit rules for getting along in the organization)

6. Climate (the feeling that is conveyed by the group related to physical layout, interactions, etc.)

7. Embedded skills (the special competencies group members display in accomplishing certain tasks)

8. Habits of thinking/mental models (the shared cognitive frame or "ways of thinking" used by members)

9. Shared meanings (emergent understandings shared by group members)

10. Root metaphors or integrating symbols (the ideas, feelings, and images developed by the group to characterize itself)

Now let's examine another school and its culture from Schein's perspective.

At Howell Junior High School, a negative culture exists. When teachers are asked to share their mission, many report that they want to get through the year and "keep the zoo under control." Many of the teachers at Howell have been assigned there from other buildings; the school is seen as a dumping ground for ineffective teachers. The staff has an informal award that is given each month (at an off-site location) to the teacher that has encountered the most difficult situation and put the person causing the situation in his or her place. Teachers at the school rarely attend

---

1. From *Organizational Culture and Leadership* (pp. 8–10), by E. Schein, 2004, San Francisco: Jossey-Bass. Copyright 2004 by John Wiley & Sons, Inc. Reprinted with permission.

extracurricular activities, and those new teachers who do are quickly confronted by veteran staff members and "set straight." The teachers rarely volunteer for committees and task forces, so the principal, Elana, has to assign people to these roles. In staff meetings, very little actual work is completed (outside of teachers correcting student homework). The teacher evaluation process is met with resistance; teachers talk about the frivolous suggestions for improvement that they receive from Elana. After the contracted duty day is over, there is a race to the parking lot.

The example may seem to be a little extreme, but as you can see, negative behaviors have become institutionalized at Howell. The negative culture illustrates several of the 10 aspects pointed out by Schein earlier and is the result of several years of negative climate components going uncorrected. Elana has her work cut out for her as the principal of this school and faces the possibility of falling into the negative culture of the school herself.

RAPPORT, TRUST, CLIMATE, CULTURE, AND THEIR INTERRELATIONSHIP

Rapport, trust, and climate are crucial aspects of the success of a school and its principal and administrative team. The aspects of rapport, trust, and climate work together to assist in the development of a school's culture. Let's take a brief look at these elements and their interrelationships:

Rapport. Rapport relates to the interpersonal relationship between two parties on a moment-to-moment basis. Since rapport is based on moment-to-moment interactions, the strategies that help to build rapport tend to be interpersonal in nature; examples include looking at other people while you are speaking to them, sincerely smiling when something interests you, showing personal regard to another, etc.

Trust. Trust relates to a group's understanding that both the group itself and the individuals within the group are reliable (Tarter as reported in Kochanek, 2005, p. 7). Trust is built on the summation of many experiences with a person. The elements of integrity, reliability, honesty, competence, and personal regard work together to help you develop a sense of trust with another person.

Climate. Climate is an aspect that relates to the day-to-day tone or feeling in an organization. The leader of a school helps to set the climate of the organization through words and actions. Climate is important, because it leads to the establishment of the culture of the organization.

SOURCE: Eller & Carlson (2008).

The elements of rapport, trust, and climate are vehicles that you can have an impact on as the principal and ultimately begin to shape the school's culture. While you may not be able to impact the culture in the short term, you can build rapport, develop trusting relationships, and implement strategies to nurture a positive school culture. Let's look at some of the elements we just introduced in more detail.

THE IMPORTANCE OF TRUST

In *The Leadership Challenge* (2007), authors Kouzes and Posner discuss many principles essential to excellent leadership. The book is currently in its fourth printing, after having first come on the market in 1987. The book is unique in its content, because most of the principles outlined in it are based on research. Since 1987, the authors have been asking people to respond to a survey outlining important characteristics of leaders. Over the past 25 years, the following four leadership attributes have been rated the highest:

- Honest
- Forward-looking
- Inspiring
- Competent (Kouzes and Posner, 2007, p. 29)

How can principals utilize this information and begin to impact school climate and ultimately the culture of a school? Here are some suggestions:

Honest (Sample Strategies)

- Be honest but diplomatic when looking at needed areas of improvement at your school. People would rather know up front about situations than find out about them through the grapevine or be surprised later.

- When parents call with complaints of negative information about teachers, let the teacher know about the call. Share with the teacher that what you are sharing is just the parent's perspective and that you are not accusing him or her related to the parental perception. Tell the teacher that you just wanted him or her to know in case something else comes up as a result of the situation.

- When evaluating teachers, be careful to make sure you provide accurate feedback. Don't overpraise or be overcritical when conferencing or providing feedback to your teachers.

Forward-Thinking (Sample Strategies)

- Your staff members will be looking to you to help them see beyond the present moment and look into the future. Some people call this behavior "sharing the vision." As you talk about the future, provide clear pictures of how things will be based on the strengths and limitations of the school.

• When dealing with issues that come up from time to time at the school, be careful not to revisit the past all the time. Don't always rely on what's been done in the past; clearly communicate that you are interested in talking about what can be done in the present with the situation.

• At staff meetings, allow for plenty of time to brainstorm lots of possible solutions to presented problems. Ask staff members to hold off in judging the ideas that are brainstormed until all of the possible ideas are shared. This will allow you to get lots of ideas on the table for consideration and help the group to focus on the future rather than the past related to problems they may encounter.

Inspiring (Sample Strategies)

• Effective principals know how to make people feel good about themselves and where they work. Look for opportunities to point out the positive attributes of the people you work with and the school you lead. As you inspire people, remember to be honest and realistic. What you say to inspire others will become reality if they trust and believe you.

• Share the context of potential problems, and help people see their place in relation to the big picture. This will help you motivate and inspire people to move beyond the negative attributes some problems bring to the school.

• At the beginning of new projects or initiatives, plan for the culminating celebration that will occur when the project is completed. Many organizations fail to plan for celebrations and end up skipping this important part of the success and inspiration of a group.

• Allow people to get to know you and see that you are real. At times, letting your guard down in an appropriate manner can inspire your staff members to do the same. Allowing people to see "inside" of you brings the important human element to the workplace.

Competent (Sample Strategies)

• As the leader of a school, you need to be seen as competent in your own professional practice. Seek feedback about your strengths and limitations so you can continue to grow and learn as a leader. You may not know how to do everything perfectly, but people will come to respect your skills if they see you are growing and learning.

• Let your staff members know when you are involved in training and development. This message communicates that you are competent and confident enough to remain a learner while on the job. Share what you think is appropriate related to your growth with staff members at meetings and seminars.

• Focus on what you do best, and seek help from others when you face tasks or jobs that challenge you.

• Make sure that the basic structures are in place for the orderly and efficient operation of the school to take place. People will see you as competent if the office operates in an efficient manner, meetings are scheduled in advance, there are processes in place to handle common situations, and the school is orderly.

BUILDING AND SUSTAINING ORGANIZATIONAL TRUST

The area of establishing and building trust is a key component in developing a positive school climate and ultimately beginning to impact the culture of your school.

In the book, *Building Trust for Better Schools*, author Julie Reed Kochanek shares the following finding: "The latest research on trust in school has even demonstrated a positive relationship between trust and school effectiveness, making a connection between the growth of trust and organizational changes, which can lead to improved educational outcomes for students. (Bryk & Schneider, 2002, Goddard, Tschannen-Moran, & Hoy, 2001; Hoy, Tarter & Witkoskie, 1992)" (2005, pp. 6–7). Since trust relates so closely to climate, the development of it positively impacts student achievement. What is experienced by the teachers is indirectly transmitted to the students.

In *Leadership and the New Science* (1995), Wheatley contends that values and behaviors have a way of being transmitted throughout organizations. If a value or behavior is exhibited in one part of the organization, it will show up somewhere else even if the two parts of the organization are in limited contact. Your efforts to genuinely increase trust in your school will ultimately result in improving the school climate for the teachers, which will result in an improved climate and learning environment for the students.

Kochanek provides additional information about trust in the following:

> The body of work coming out of Ohio State University from Hoy and his colleagues (Tarter et al., 1989, p. 295) defines trust as a group understanding that both the group itself and the individuals within the group are reliable. Further conceptual study from this group led to a description of the five components of faculty trust: benevolence, reliability, competence, honesty, and openness (Hoy & Tschannen-Moran, 1999). (2005, pp. 6–7)

STRATEGIES TO BUILD TRUST AND IMPACT SCHOOL CLIMATE[2]

- Develop open communication about roles and expectations.
- Be clear in defining work expectations (work "contracts").
- Show integrity by sharing your beliefs related to what is best for children and then following through on those beliefs.
- Show personal regard when dealing with others.
- Generate familiarity among diverse groups (socially, ethnically, etc.) by providing opportunities to communicate and interact through social exchanges.
- Lower the perception of vulnerability that some groups may feel in interactions.
- Engage in simple activities to build a base for more complex activities later.
- Follow through on what you promise; avoid overpromising.

SUMMARY

The terms *climate* and *culture* are sometimes used interchangeably by educators. Keep in mind the differences between the two terms and how they impact your school. Climate refers to the feeling tone of your school. Climate is more easily changed than culture. School culture, on the other hand, refers to a deeper, more embedded aspect of your school. The culture of a school includes observable and unobservable components such as formal practices, artifacts (or products), and the informal rules of the organization. Culture can be difficult to impact because of its more permanent, embedded nature.

As you review the major concepts from this chapter, reflect on the following questions:

- Why is climate so important for the operation of a good school?
- What are some examples of positive climate attributes?
- What processes do people go through in developing trusting relationships? How do people manage these processes?
- How does climate work to impact school culture? What are examples of items you could examine that would give you an idea of the culture of a school?

In this first chapter, we have provided you with a brief overview of the general concepts of school climate and culture. This was important, because as a principal, you need to be able to identify aspects of both climate and

---

2. From *Building Trust for Better Schools* (pp. 7–32), by J. Kochanek, 2005, Thousand Oaks, CA: Corwin. Copyright 2005 by Corwin. Adapted with permission.

culture in your school before you can begin to assess them and make plans for their improvement. In Chapter 2, you will learn the process of diagnosing your school's climate and culture, beginning to develop a plan for making positive adjustments to the climate, and then impacting the larger school culture. Being able to identify the existing state and then develop a sound plan to address these issues is essential for your success as a principal trying to impact climate and culture. The process will help you as you review the remaining chapters in the book dealing with ideas and strategies.

2

Diagnosing the Present Climate and Culture of Your School

Kory, the new principal of Washington High School, knew that her school had some internal problems. After all, that is why she was going to be the third principal there in five years. She had been told by the superintendent that there were relationship problems at the school and that some parents in the community had expressed concerns about the attitudes of some of the teachers. Kory was prepared to deal with these issues, because she had worked to turn around her previous school, a middle school in another nearby community. Washington High School presented a more complex challenge than she had faced in the past. She had a feeling of at least some of the issues she needed to address, but how would she get a more accurate read on the problems and strengths of Washington, so she could target her improvement efforts? What kinds of instruments and processes would be available for her to use to gather accurate data? Once these data were gathered and analyzed, what kind of improvement plan could she develop to get Washington High School moving in the right direction toward improving first the climate and then the culture? How could she start the year off on the right foot and implement the right strategies to help the Washington staff to improve?

Kory faced a task not uncommon in educational leadership: how to get a school to begin the process of healing and improving its climate. The leader is the primary person responsible for the improvement and maintenance of the school climate. As we learned in Chapter 1, the climate of a school has a large impact on the educational learning environment. Several researchers contend that the culture of a school is impossible to change, but keep in mind that as you begin to institutionalize school climate changes, they have an impact on the culture over time. Kory knows she needs to take the bull by the horns and begin to work on improving the climate and ultimately the culture of Washington High School.

The diagnosis of the present climate and culture of a school is crucial to the success of administrators seeking to impact these important elements. Once the strengths and limitations of these components are identified, a clear and well-developed plan needs to be implemented to ensure that the school gets on the right path to improvement. This plan needs to be as well developed as the academic improvement plans that principals have become so accustomed to writing and implementing in relation to academic improvement initiatives.

ABOUT THIS CHAPTER

In this chapter, we will provide you with the tools and strategies to diagnose the climate and culture of your school and then develop and implement a plan that works toward the improvement of these areas. As you read this chapter, you will learn the following:

- Informal strategies to gather data related to school climate and culture
- Surveys and checklists that are available for your use in gathering data
- Templates to assist in the planning and implementation of a climate and culture improvement effort

As you read this chapter, continue to think about how these strategies may work in your setting. Select those strategies and ideas that will help your school be successful.

INFORMAL DIAGNOSTIC STRATEGIES

Many principals use informal strategies to diagnose the climate and culture of their schools. For the purpose of this book, we are calling strategies that utilize readily available data at the school informal. The term informal in no way denotes that these data sources are any less important or valid than other sources of information. We have classified these strategies into three classifications, teacher interviews, focus groups, and observations/artifact collection.

Teacher Interviews

Principals who conduct individual teacher interviews find out a lot about the climate and culture of their schools. In conducting these interviews, it's important to set the right tone and use good strategies that allow people to share their perceptions of the school. While interviewing teachers may sound easy, there are some things to keep in mind as you implement the strategy. In this section we will discuss ideas related to opportunities for interviewing teachers and thoughts for question construction, and we will provide sample templates to assist you if you choose to implement one of these strategies.

Interviewing teachers before the start of the year

Even though this strategy is discussed in Chapter 3, we feel it is important to mention it here as well. A good time to talk with teachers about the climate and culture of the school is when they outside of the school setting. From our experiences, we have found teachers to be more relaxed and open when they are outside of the school. Their level of openness can provide you with an opportunity to really find out their thoughts and ideas.

We have contacted teachers about the opportunity to get together to talk about the school before the start of the year using either a letter or a phone call. Some principals contact teachers when they are new to the building to find out people's perception of the climate/culture. Figure 2.1 shows a sample of a letter we have used to introduce them to this idea:

Figure 2.1   Sample Interview/Introduction Letter for a New Principal

---

(Date)

Dear Staff,

My name is (Name) and I am the new principal of (Name) School. I am excited to be working at your school. (Name) School has a great reputation in the (Community name) metro area. I am looking forward to a great year together.

I believe in a very close and professional working relationship between the staff and me at the school. This relationship helps us to work together and accomplish great things as a team. Because of the importance of our work as a team, we need to have an opportunity to get to know each other. I would like to meet with each of you personally to share some of my background plus get to know you. I am in the process of setting up times for us to meet during the weeks of August 6th through

---

(Continued)

(Continued)

August 30th. I will be setting aside 20-minute slots. In these time slots I want to tell you a little bit about my background and me, find out more about you, and see what your hopes and dreams are professionally and for the future of (Name) School. In schools where I have been a principal in the past, the staff really enjoyed this opportunity and found that it helped to set the stage for our work together at the school.

Since I will be talking with each of you personally, I would like to set up these meetings so that they fit your schedule. Please call (Secretary name and number) to set up a meeting time and location. We could meet at the school or an alternative location if you would prefer. I look forward to meeting each of you personally in the next few weeks.

Have a great summer!

Sincerely,

In other situations, principals conduct interviews of their teachers after they have been at the building for a time. Their interest in gathering teacher perceptions may be the result of noticing a steady deterioration in the school climate. The same type of interviews can be conducted if you are an existing principal of a school. Figure 2.2 shows a sample letter that can be sent to inform teachers of your intent to talk with them over the summer in relation to the school climate/culture:

Figure 2.2   Sample Interview Letter for Existing Principals

(Date)

Dear Staff,

Last spring, in our staff meetings we began to talk about ideas to improve the working environment of our school. One of the strategies we talked about was having me conduct a series of individual interviews with each of you to gain your perspective on the work environment and climate of our school.

I am in the process of setting up times for us to meet during the weeks of August 6th through August 30th. I will be setting aside 20-minute slots for these meetings. In these time slots I want to get your perspective on the working climate and see what your hopes and dreams are for the future of (Name) School. I plan to use the information I gather in these personal meetings to begin to develop a plan to positively impact our working climate.

Since I will be talking with each of you personally, I would like to set up these meetings so that they fit your schedule. Please call (Secretary name and number) to set up a meeting time and location. We could meet at the school or an alternative location if you would prefer. I look forward to meeting with each of you personally in the next few weeks.

Have a great summer!

Sincerely,

(Name of principal)

Another strategy we have found helpful is to just call teachers in the summer to share your intent to talk with them about the school. When making these calls, it's a good idea to have some sort of script or talking guide in mind so that you are giving each person a similar message. Figure 2.3 is a sample of a script we have used when calling teachers to meet with them over the summer:

Figure 2.3   Phone Call Script for a New Principal

"Hello, this is (Name) and I'm calling to see if you have some time to get together with me to talk."

"I'm meeting with all of the teachers to let them get to know a little about me since I'm new to the building, and I'd also like to find out more about you."

"I'd like to meet you somewhere or talk here at the school for about 30 minutes."

"I'm interested in your opinions and ideas related to the climate of our school."

"The thoughts you share with me are important, and I will use the information I gather to begin to make my plans for the upcoming school year."

"Thank you for taking the time to talk to me; I look forward to meeting you and hearing your thoughts related to (Name) School."

Obviously, you need to use a script and words that make the most sense for you. The script we provided in Figure 2.3 was developed to provide some guidance as you move forward with this strategy. Be sure to use words and a process that is natural for you.

We have found it important when dealing with situations where the climate has deteriorated to provide consistency and fair treatment of all staff. If you deviate too far from a script, some teachers will receive different information about the interview. Some teachers will tell their colleagues that they got a different message, which can pit people against each other.

Interviewing teachers during the year

Another opportunity to find out teacher perceptions related to the climate and culture is during the year, when teachers are immersed in school. We worked with a principal who made it a practice to set up interviews with his staff members during the midterm period of the first quarter of school. During this time, he asked his teachers to talk about their perceptions of the climate and culture of the school. Because of the size of the staff, these interviews took a couple of weeks to complete, but he analyzed the information he gathered from them and shared it at a staff meeting early in the second quarter. His timing worked well, because the interviews were conducted after the year was underway, and all of the start-up chaos had passed.

Exit or end-of-the-year interviews

Another good opportunity to interview teachers and gather information related to their perceptions of the climate and culture of the school happens at the end of the year during the checkout process. We find that at this time of the year, teachers tend to be more relaxed and open, since the pressures of teaching and grading are past them. As teachers check out, you can ask them a few questions that give you valuable information related to the climate and culture.

Focus Groups

Several of our colleagues have used focus groups in finding out perceptions of their school climate and culture. These colleagues have implemented their focus groups in a variety of ways. One principal formed a focus group of teachers and spent two hours with them after the school day at an offsite location. Another principal involved parent and community members in small focus groups to find out how the school was doing. These small groups of two or three community members came in and met with her throughout the day in scheduled sessions. She got some very good insights from working with them.

When working with focus groups, it's important to design the process so that you get the maximum information from the group during their time with you. Keep the following ideas in mind as you prepare to work with focus groups:

• At the beginning of the focus group session, let the group know what you are hoping (in general) to gain from their participation.

• Consider giving focus group members copies of the questions you will be asking in the session at the start of the session. Allow them to have a few minutes to write down their thoughts and answers related to the questions before you start the group discussion. This practice allows them to think of ideas and answers, so they can fully participate in the group process.

• Start out with more general or open-ended questions; then move to more specific questions as the discussion unfolds.

• Start with a set of predetermined questions to use as a script. Be sure to get information related to your needs before allowing the group to go off on its own direction. If you are meeting with multiple groups, you will want to make sure that you stay close to your script, so you can get similar information from all of your groups. If you allow each group to do its own thing, you will not have enough similar data that you can use to make decisions about your improvement plan.

Online Surveys

Depending on the level of trust between you and your teachers (or between your teachers and administration in general), you may not have much success gathering information from them using personal interviews.

You may want to consider asking your questions using an online survey instrument instead of conducting live interviews. As you think about this strategy, you will want to develop a survey that draws out the kind of information that you need to gather in order to develop your improvement plan. Keep the following in mind as you develop your survey:

- Think about what you want to learn about in relation to the climate and culture of your school. Focus on the specific aspects that you want to explore in more depth.

- Decide on the type of survey you want to administer. Do you want people to respond to open-ended questions, or do you want to provide them with choices and ask them to select from a set of possible responses?

- After you have developed a preliminary set of survey questions, ask a group of representatives from your target group to read and share their reactions to the survey items. This process helps you to make sure that what you think you are asking is what participants think you are asking. If the perceptions are similar to what you intended in designing the questions, you have a good survey.

- Examine the length of the survey. Most people don't want to respond to a large number of questions. Make sure that every question is essential for your data gathering. A rule of thumb we like to use is to limit surveys of this nature to a page (on the computer screen) or about 10 questions.

Electronic survey tools

There are many electronic survey tools on the market these days. Your school district may have one of them loaded on its server as a part of a software bundle. We have used the survey tool Survey Monkey to do a lot of our work. Survey Monkey has many features and is easy to use. It has a free membership, and you are able to buy more comprehensive memberships on a monthly basis. The URL for the site is www.surveymonkey.com. Look over the site, and see what you think about how it may help you gather data about your school and staff members.

Observations and Artifact Collection

Recall the list of common attributes of groups (Schein, 2004) that we introduced in Chapter 1 (see p. 8). Since these aspects work together to define the culture of a school, you can use them to diagnose your present school culture. We have designed a template based on the aspects outlined by Schein. You may find this template valuable as you begin to diagnose your present school culture. In order to use the template, look for or gather data or artifacts that fit into the various categories listed in the template. After you have completed the gathering of data or artifacts, analyze what you have gathered to gain a better understanding of the culture of your school.

Figure 2.4 contains a blank template that you may use in diagnosing your own school. In Figures 2.5a and 2.5b, completed examples are provided.

Figure 2.4 School Culture Diagnosis Template

School Cultural Aspect	Evidence Gathered (through observations, interviews, reviewing artifacts, etc.)	Description of Culture Related to Evidence (What is this culture like in this area?)
Observed behavioral regularities—What kinds of language do people use? How do they interact in formal and informal settings?		
Group norms—What kinds of formal and informal rules seem to govern meetings and work relationships?		
Espoused values—What kinds of values does the group use in achieving its goals? What are the group's goals and aspirations?		
Formal philosophy—How does the group view and treat stakeholders?		
Rules of the game—What does it take to get along here and be successful?		
Climate—What is the physical layout of the work environments? What is the feel of the organization?		
Embedded skills—What special skills are required or must be developed to be successful in this environment?		
Habits of thinking and mental models—How do people process and problem-solve here? What assumptions guide their thinking?		
Shared meanings—What informal language or slang exists here? What inside information do people need to know in order to "get it"?		
Root metaphors or integrating symbols—What images or icons seem to describe the group or help them relate to each other in their work here?		

SOURCE: Adapted from Eller & Carlson (2008).

To give you a better idea of how this template might work in an actual school, we provide a completed template in Figure 2.5a. This figure contains examples of positive culture attributes.

In contrast to Figure 2.5a, the completed template in Figure 2.5b contains examples of negative culture attributes.

Figure 2.5a	School Culture Diagnosis Template With All Positive Examples

School Cultural Aspect	Evidence Gathered (through observations, interviews, reviewing artifacts, etc.)	Description of Culture Related to Evidence (What is this culture like in this area?)
Observed behavioral regularities—What kinds of language do people use? How do they interact in formal and informal settings?	• Many teachers feel they make a difference in their students' learning. • Staff members meet to talk about student learning. • When a staff member encounters a problem, others assist the staff member in positive ways.	• Supportive culture • Optimistic culture
Group norms—What kinds of formal and informal rules seem to govern meetings and work relationships?	• Senior staff members assist new teachers through mentoring and guidance. • Teachers openly invite ideas from all staff. • Group meetings are collaborative and focus on resolving issues.	• Collaborative • "We value your opinion." • A "we" versus a "me" culture
Espoused values— What kinds of values does the group use in achieving its goals? What are the group's goals and aspirations?	• Relationships extend beyond the workplace. • The group takes pride in dealing with difficult situations.	• Culture of togetherness. • "We need to look at problems with fresh eyes."
Formal philosophy— How does the group view and treat stakeholders?	• Parents are involved in major school committees. • Teachers initiate two-way communication with parents.	• Stakeholder opinions are valued. • Parents are seen as partners in the education process.
Rules of the game— What does it take to get along here and be successful?	• Mentors share ideas and strategies with new teachers. • A problem-solving process has been formalized at the school.	• High trust is developed. • Supportive culture • Positive problem resolution strategies

(Continued)

(Continued)

School Cultural Aspect	Evidence Gathered (through observations, interviews, reviewing artifacts, etc.)	Description of Culture Related to Evidence (What is this culture like in this area?)
Climate—What is the physical layout of the work environments? What is the feel of the organization?	• Classroom doors are open; teachers in halls interact positively with students and others. • Front entrance of building is bright and inviting.	• Highly collaborative • High-energy culture
Climate—What is the physical layout of the work environments? What is the feel of the organization?	• Classroom doors are open; teachers in halls interact positively with students and others. • Front entrance of building is bright and inviting.	• Highly collaborative • High-energy culture
Embedded skills— What special skills are required or must be developed to be successful in this environment?	• Teachers are organized into small support groups. • Conflict resolution processes are used. • Group has adopted operating norms.	• Supportive environment • Conflict is a natural process. • Collaborative culture
Habits of thinking and mental models—How do people process and problem-solve here? What assumptions guide their thinking?	• Many ideas are suggested when staff is dealing with problems. • A formal problem-solving process has been adopted. • Decisions are based on what is best for the students.	• Decisions based on data and information are valued. • Focus is on the students.
Shared meanings— What informal language or slang exists here? What inside information do people need to know in order to "get it"?	• Positive mentors are provided for new staff members. • People take pride in rituals used in the school. People also take pride in the school they work in.	• Open and transparent • Pride in the workplace
Root metaphors or integrating symbols— What images or icons seem to describe the group or help them relate to each other in their work here?	• Teachers refer to their classrooms as learning centers. • Classroom procedures are designed by teachers and students together. • There is regular recognition for staff members who help each other.	• Positive and inviting • Hopeful • Energizing culture

SOURCE: Adapted from Eller & Carlson (2008).

Figure 2.5b School Culture Diagnosis Template With All Negative Examples

School Cultural Aspect	Evidence Gathered (through observations, interviews, reviewing artifacts, etc.)	Description of Culture Related to Evidence (What is this culture like in this area?)
Observed behavioral regularities—What kinds of language do people use? How do they interact in formal and informal settings?	• Many teachers say "These students can't learn." • Staff members meet infrequently. • When a staff member encounters a problem, others say, "I'm glad it's not me."	• Nonsupportive culture • Blaming culture
Group norms—What kinds of formal and informal rules seem to govern meetings and work relationships?	• Senior staff members watch new staff to make sure they don't "show up" others. • Junior staff members are reluctant to ask questions or suggest new ideas. • A few people "run" staff meetings, not allowing others to share ideas.	• Controlling • You have to earn your place here. • Only a few deserve an opinion.
Espoused values—What kinds of values does the group use in achieving its goals? What are the group's goals and aspirations?	• The group goals seem to be related to hierarchy and control. • Experience and longevity are valued.	• Not receptive to new ideas • The old ways are best.
Formal philosophy—How does the group view and treat stakeholders?	• Parents are not welcome and kept at bay.	• Low level of collaboration • Hierarchy and control
Rules of the game—What does it take to get along here and be successful?	• Keep your head down. • Cover yourself.	• Low trust • Unclear accountability • Blaming culture
Climate—What is the physical layout of the work environments? What is the feel of the organization?	• Teachers all have offices with closed doors; the windows on the offices are covered with paper, so no one can see in them. • Halls are dark and dull	• Low collaboration • Low-energy culture
Embedded skills—What special skills are required or must be developed to be successful in this environment?	• Assertiveness • Being able to handle conflict • Self-protection	• Take care of yourself. • Blame others for your problems.

(Continued)

(Continued)

School Cultural Aspect	Evidence Gathered (through observations, interviews, reviewing artifacts, etc.)	Description of Culture Related to Evidence (What is this culture like in this area?)
Habits of thinking and mental models—How do people process and problem-solve here? What assumptions guide their thinking?	• The first suggestion from a meeting is normally implemented. • The easiest and most straightforward idea is usually selected. • The convenience of the teachers is the primary consideration in selecting a plan to implement.	• Do what's easiest. • Focus on the staff, not the students.
Shared meanings—What informal language or slang exists here? What inside information do people need to know in order to "get it"?	• Frequently, new staff members are told, "You just don't understand" or "You're too idealistic; we'll give you some more time to learn" or "That's not the way we do things around here." • Nicknames are used for students.	• Controlling • Blaming
Root metaphors or integrating symbols— What images or icons seem to describe the group or help them relate to each other in their work here?	• Negative teachers refer to their classrooms as the "war zone." • Most classroom rules and regulations are prohibitive or punitive in nature. • There is a staff award for surviving the most difficult parent.	• Negative • Hopeless • Survival

SOURCE: Adapted from Eller & Carlson (2008).

FORMAL OR STRUCTURED DIAGNOSTIC INSTRUMENTS

Since the areas of school climate and culture are so crucial to the academic success of a school, there are several formal or structured surveys on the market. These instruments are normally research based and try to find information related to people's thoughts and perceptions. We will highlight a few here.

Hoy and Hoy (2009) devote an entire chapter of their book entitled *Instructional Leadership: A Research-Based Guide to Learning in Schools* to the topics of school climate and culture. In Chapter 9 of the book, they discuss two instruments that they have developed and tested.

The Organizational Health Inventory (OHI) asks staff members to rate various elements according to the elements' presence or absence in the school. The OHI instrument can be found at www.coe.ohio-state.edu/whoy. There are versions for administration in elementary, middle, and high schools. Dr. Wayne Hoy has given permission for schools to use the instrument for school improvement. The basic instructions for administration of the instrument are listed on the Web site along with directions for scoring and interpreting the results.

The Organizational Climate Description Questionnaire (OCDQ) asks staff members to rate interactions. The questionnaire is also available at www.coe.ohio-state.edu/whoy. Dr. Hoy also says that the questionnaire may be downloaded and used for school improvement purposes for no charge. Specific administration, scoring, and interpretation instructions are listed on the website.

The Culture Audit

Dr. Rebecca M. Bustamante, professor at Sam Houston State University, has developed a "Culture Audit" that can be used by schools in their quest to diagnose their school cultures. The instrument is currently being tested for validity, but it is worth looking at if you are interested. It is housed on the National Council of Professors of Educational Administration (NCPEA) Web site. The address is www.ncpea.net. Once you are on the site, click on Connexions, and then enter "Culture Audit" in the search field in the upper right corner.

This instrument covers a variety of aspects of school culture and asks participants to rate several items on a scale from 1 to 5 based on their frequency in the school. Since the instrument is on the Connexions database, it will be updated as it is refined, so you will always be able to access the latest version for your use.

PLANNING TEMPLATES

Once you start to gain an understanding of the present issues related to the climate and eventually the culture of the school, it's time to begin to think about planning interventions. Think about climate and culture interventions in the same light as you would academic interventions. Climate changes will take the same amount of focus, work, and follow-up that your other school improvement planning takes.

Even though climate and culture may take as much planning and follow-up as other school improvement interventions, we have found it to be important to keep the plans as simple and straightforward as possible. If your climate and culture intervention plans get too complicated, it will be easy for people in your building to get confused. Keep the following ideas in mind as you begin to develop your planning to improve the school climate and culture:

• Utilize data from a variety of sources in developing a direction for your plan; make sure that you have an accurate "read" on these aspects of the school before you get started.

• Even though a plan to improve the climate and culture of your school is as important as an academic improvement plan, you may not be able to publicly share it as you would an academic improvement plan. People at your building may be more sensitive to certain elements or assertions outlined in the plan because of the highly emotional nature of climate and culture issues. People in your building may also be in denial or blame others on the staff for the problems that the plan is designed to address. You may need to have a simple, straightforward plan that is shared with the entire staff and then have a more complex plan that you use yourself to track your efforts behind the scenes.

• Be sure to think about the vision for the final plan, and incorporate this aspect in your planning. If you are completing the plan, think about what the school will look like once your plan has been implemented and accomplished. Use this vision as a way to measure your efforts.

The planning template provided in Figure 2.6 is one we have found to be helpful as we have planned climate and culture interventions in schools. In Figure 2.7 we provide an example template to show you what the template looks like once it is filled out.

From the example, you can see that the planning is fairly specific for each of the goal areas. As we said before, there are certain elements of the plan that may be made public or shared with staff members, while there are other aspects that you may not want to share. You have to decide on your openness based on the level of trust and rapport you have with your staff. Some principals find it important to let their teachers know right up front their concerns about climate issues, while other principals are more comfortable gradually releasing certain aspects of their plans to address climate and culture issues over time. You have to decide what's best for you. In any case, you may find the planning template and examples helpful as you begin the process of working to improve the climate and culture of your school.

SUMMARY

Diagnosing the school climate and culture is an essential task for principals and building leaders. While the climate of a school may be related to the "feel" or more day-to-day aspects of a school, the culture relates to deeper or more permanent aspects. In this chapter, we have provided ideas and strategies for you to use in diagnosing these two aspects of your

(text continues on page 32)

Figure 2.6 Planning Template

General Goal: _____

Climate/Culture Area of Focus: _____

Team Members: _____

1. General Goal Statement	2. Present Level of Functioning	3. Gap Between Present Level of Functioning and Desired Level of Functioning	4. Strategies Needed to Be Successful With Goal Area	5. Timeline for Implementation	6. People Responsible for Strategies or Goal Area	7. Vision of What School Will Look Like if the Goal Is Attained

SOURCE: From *Effective Group Facilitation in Education: How to Energize Meetings and Manage Difficult Groups*, (p. 151), by J. Eller, 2004, Thousand Oaks, CA: Corwin. Copyright 2004 by Corwin. Reprinted with permission.

Figure 2.7 Example Planning Template

General Goal: To improve the climate and ultimately the culture of Achievement Middle School so that staff members see the school as a positive place to work, students see the school as a good place to learn, and parents perceive it as a good place to send their children.

Climate/Culture Area of Focus: This plan will include the following focus areas:

1. The front entrance of the school will be restructured so that it is welcoming to staff, students, and parents.

2. Staff member relations will be improved through increased communication, conflict resolution, and clear expectations.

3. Staff members will get to know each other on a personal basis through the use of team-building activities at selected staff meetings.

Team Members: [Team member names] will be involved in the front entrance project. [Principal's name] will manage the staff member relations subgoal. [Team member names] will be involved in the team-building subgoal.

1. General Goal Statement	2. Present Level of Functioning	3. Gap Between Present Level of Functioning and Desired Level of Functioning	4. Strategies Needed to Be Successful With Goal Area	5. Timeline for Implementation	6. People Responsible for Strategies or Goal Area	7. Vision of What School Will Look Like if the Goal Is Attained
Improve front entrance.	Area is dark and unwelcoming.	Adequate lighting, posted student work, a place for a greeter, and a welcoming tone are all missing.	• The area needs to be repainted. • Additional lighting needs to be installed. • Student work needs to be posted; trophy cases need to be installed. • Volunteer greeters need to be identified and trained.	• In August, the hall will be painted and trophy cases installed. • By September, greeters will be secured and trained. • By October, student work will be identified and displayed.	[Names]	The entrance will be well lit and inviting; someone will be in the area to welcome faculty, students, and visitors to the building.

1. General Goal Statement	2. Present Level of Functioning	3. Gap Between Present Level of Functioning and Desired Level of Functioning	4. Strategies Needed to Be Successful With Goal Area	5. Timeline for Implementation	6. People Responsible for Strategies or Goal Area	7. Vision of What School Will Look Like if the Goal Is Attained
Improve staff relations.	Staff members dig in on issues and fail to listen to each other. Relationships suffer because of this condition.	There is a lack of a process to resolve issues in groups. People get mad and avoid each other.	• Staff members need to be made aware of the conflict issues and their impact on relationships. • Staff need to be taught suspension of opinion and practice its use.	• In the August staff meeting, the principal will present a session about types of conflict and their impact on schools. • In early September, the principal will present a session on suspension of opinion to the staff and allow them time to practice the skill.	[Principal]	Staff members will use conflict resolution strategies when engaging in conversation.

SOURCE: Adapted from Eller (2004).

(continued from page 28)

school. As you move forward to determine the climate and culture of your school, think about the following:

- Using what you've learned in this chapter, how might you go about gathering data to diagnose your school's climate and culture?
- What components do you need to keep in mind in your planning to begin to address climate and culture issues?
- How might interviews and focus groups help you as you as you try to diagnose your school's climate and culture?

The information in this chapter was designed to assist you as you begin to get to know more about the climate and culture of your school. Once you understand the state of your school, it's time to begin to select the activities and strategies that you need in order to first impact the school's climate and then the culture. The remainder of this book contains a wide variety of strategies and ideas that you can use to begin to move your school in a more positive and productive direction.

3

Building the Foundation for Success

Les, the new principal at Mountain View Elementary, had heard that the work climate was negative at his school. Since the climate had been negative for a number of years, it had impacted the culture as well. As Les talked with teachers during the summer before the school year started, he heard comments that helped reinforce that many of his teachers did not enjoy working at Mountain View. Les went back to the school and started to think about what he had learned as a result of his conversations. As he entered the front door of the school, he noticed that the paint on the doors was peeling and the planters there were filled with weeds. The office staff area was cluttered and the staff was crammed into a space that was much too small for the three office staff that supported the school. He started to look around the school and found that the area where most teachers entered the building was equally depressing. When entering the building, the teachers had to walk near an old dumpster, and the entrance door paint was also peeling. The entrance looked depressing to Les.

He immediately met with his custodial staff and worked with them to develop a plan to clean up the front entrance and paint the doors and the door frames. He had the custodial staff replace the rugs there and wax the floor in the front entrance to the building. Les contacted the parent-teacher organization (PTO) president and talked to her about a project to clean up the planters in the front of the building. The PTO purchased new plants and cleaned up the beds in one day. When Les had met earlier with the front office staff, they had expressed frustration with their present accommodations. Les worked with them to relocate two of the people to areas where they could have more space plus be out of the front entrance where distractions had previously kept them from getting their work completed. He assisted the staff member remaining in the area to organize her files and store items in another location that were not always needed on a regular basis. Her area had not been clean and well organized, and the reorganization and storage made it more inviting for her as well as for others. Les contacted the trash company and asked them to replace the dumpster and move it about 20 feet to the right of where it had been. This moved it away from the back door and improved that entrance. He had the area cleaned and painted, so that entrance was also inviting for the staff.

Les had many other ideas in mind to clean up the facility but waited until he finished his meetings with staff members before he initiated them. As teachers came in to work in the rooms, several made it a point to stop by the office and tell Les about their happiness with the changes. They commented that the changes he had made so far really made the building feel more professional and inviting. Les took teachers around to the various areas that had been cleaned and painted so they could see how this improved the looks of the school. At the first staff meeting in the fall, several teachers commented how fresh and inviting the building looked.

Les had made small changes in the climate. His larger goal was to improve the culture of the school. That goal would take more time and effort.

In schools, we have one luxury that many other businesses or organizations do not have. Each year our schedule begins and ends. We all have experienced the stress at the end of a school year in the spring only to come back in the fall and find that most of our staff members start with a euphoric feeling of optimism about the upcoming year. If you are a principal wanting to improve school climate, take advantage of the new emotional beginning that another school year affords you.

ABOUT THIS CHAPTER

In this chapter, we will talk briefly about the importance of starting fresh in the fall with climate improvements that will eventually lead to cultural changes in your school. We will also talk about opportunities new principals have to immediately begin to impact the climate and culture of their schools when they start interactions with staff members in the late summer or early fall. The beginning of the school year is an opportune time to really make a difference and move forward on your improvement efforts in the areas of school climate and culture.

As you read this chapter, think about the following aspects of starting the year on the right foot and building a proper foundation for success:

- What role do the office and office staff members play in establishing a positive school climate?
- What kinds of building maintenance ideas should I consider when thinking about impacting the climate and culture of my building for a great start in the fall?

- What strategies can I employ that show teachers I really care about them and appreciate the gifts they bring to my school?

The strategies and ideas contained in this chapter work to build positive relationships, which are one of the foundations of a positive school climate and culture. Enjoy these ideas and try them in your school.

WORKING WITH THE OFFICE STAFF

The office staff set the stage for the entire building. It is important to have a solid working relationship with the office staff. It is important for you as the principal of the school to set and define the expectation for the office staff and establish how you want the office to function. Some things to consider are the following:

- How the office staff greets and welcomes visitors
- How the office staff handles phone calls from other staff, parents, community, salespersons, and the media
- What the procedure is for parents and prospective students who visit the school
- How visitors will sign in, and whether visitors will wear a welcome badge
- What office hours are
- How you will use volunteers in the school
- What the welcome packet for new families will include and how it will be distributed
- Where people can obtain information about your school, such as your newsletter and information about the school and school district
- How you want to handle your appointments and meetings
- How to maintain a professional atmosphere
- How you will convey the importance of confidential information to staff, and how they will handle it
- How your school will handle forms for staff, parents, and students
- How the office staff handles fire drills, tornado drills, and lock downs
- How the office staff handles phone calls to the teachers and classrooms
- How the office staff handles communication to parents and community
- How the school calendar will look and what it will include, such as field trips, meetings, and a schedule showing when the building is in use
- How you will keep office staff current on office tasks, such as those in the areas of technology, building security, and staff development
- How you will keep office staff informed of building goals, initiatives, and programs

In order to have an office that functions well and promotes the kind of atmosphere you want for your school, you need to think through its operations and develop a plan to successfully adopt effective processes. The template in Figure 3.1 is designed to help you with the task.

In Figure 3.2 a completed template is provided so you can see how the template may look for an actual school.

It is important for you as the principal to meet with the office staff at least twice a month to address any issues or concerns and to stay connected on school activities and functions. During the office meetings, it is crucial to do staff development training and team building. It is also important to meet with your secretary on a weekly basis to review the upcoming events in the building.

STRATEGY: PLANNING AND DEVELOPING AN EFFECTIVE OFFICE STAFF

As you begin to share your vision for an effective office, you'll find that purposeful planning will help you and your office staff be more successful. It will be important for you to consider developing a clear plan. In Figure 3.3 a blank planning template is provided.

CREATING A POSITIVE PHYSICAL ENVIRONMENT FOR STAFF

STRATEGY: THROUGH THESE DOORS

College and professional athletes get a lot of special treatment in this country. Why not allow your teachers to feel special as well? We have seen principals who have taken a strategy from locker rooms and applied it to their school for staff and students. You may have noticed signs above the doors of locker rooms that say things like, "Through these doors walk the greatest wrestlers in the country" or "Home of the greatest football team in the country."

These same kinds of signs can set a great tone for your staff (and students) as they come into the buildings. Here are some examples of possible sign statements:

- "Through these doors walk the greatest teachers and students in the country."
- "These doors are the gateway to outstanding teachers and learners."
- "Welcome to [name of school] country. Be ready to learn."
- "Enter curious; leave informed."
- "The best people walk through these doors."
- "Prepare to change lives and learn when you enter."

Figure 3.1   Office Operation Identification Template

Office Procedures	Vision of Procedures in a Competent School Office
For meeting and welcoming visitors	
For handling phone calls from staff, parents, community, salespersons, and the media	
For visits to the school from parents and students	
For visitors to sign in and be issued badges	
For defining and posting office hours	
Related to volunteers in the school	
For creating and distributing welcome packets and other information sources for new families	
For scheduling appointments and meetings with the principal	
To establish and maintain a professional office atmosphere	
For handling confidential or potentially sensitive information	
For managing forms for staff, parents, and students	
For fire drills, tornado drills and lock downs	
For handling phone calls to teachers and classrooms	
For communication to parents and community	
For posting a school calendar of events such as field trips, meetings, and other occasions when the building is in use	
To keep office staff current on office tasks, such as in the areas of technology and building security, and on opportunities for staff development	
To keep office staff informed of building goals, initiatives, and programs	
Other procedures as needed	

Figure 3.2	Completed Office Operation Identification Template

Office Procedures	Vision of Procedures in a Competent School Office
For meeting and welcoming visitors	A staff member immediately greets visitors and asks if they need help. If staff members are busy with another crucial task, they tell visitors they will be with them in a moment.
For handling phone calls from staff, parents, community, salespersons, and the media	Clear written procedures have been developed and are followed by staff. These procedures include the appropriate person to route calls to if administrative assistant cannot answer question.
For visits to the school from parents and students	Clear, written procedures are in place that address appropriate situations for visits, length of time for visits, sign-in and sign-out procedures, and welcoming and orientation procedures.
For visitors to sign in and visitor badge procedures	Clear procedures are posted; office staff know who handles visitor badges, sign-in, etc.
For defining and posting office hours	Hours are posted and written in a positive manner.
Related to volunteers in the school	Procedures are clearly written to ensure seamless entry to the school. A parent volunteer sign-in book is in place. Volunteers are welcomed by staff members.
For creating and distributing welcome packets and other information sources for new families	Packets are developed and on display so families can get a copy.
For scheduling appointments and meetings with the principal	Principal has met with appropriate staff members and outlined the proper procedures for scheduling meetings and appointments. Procedures include names, contact information, topic of discussion, and other pertinent information needed by the principal to prepare for the meeting.
To establish and maintain a professional office atmosphere	Office furniture placement maximizes space and minimizes off-task conversations. Office space has ample storage and is neat and clean.

Office Procedures	Vision of Procedures in a Competent School Office
For handling confidential or potentially sensitive information	Clear procedures are written and verbally reviewed with staff on a periodic basis.
For managing forms for staff, parents, and students	Forms are placed in a shelving unit and arranged according to need.
For fire drills, tornado drills, and lock downs	Procedures are clear and posted in the office and halls near the office.
For handling phone calls to teachers and classrooms	Classroom calls are routed to voice mail during the school day; classroom phones are opened up to outside calls at the end of the school day.
For communication to parents and community	Clear, written procedures are posted at each office desk.
For posting a school calendar of events such as field trips, meetings, and other occasions when the building is in use	A large master calendar is posted that contains information related to school events.
To keep office staff current on office tasks, such as in the areas of technology and building security, and on opportunities for staff development	Periodic meetings are held to ensure that staff understand current office procedures and staff development opportunities.
To keep office staff informed of building goals, initiatives, and programs	Building goals are posted in the office. Staff meetings are periodically held to update office staff on instructional and student achievement goals.
Other procedures as needed	

Display Area for Staff Photos and Awards

The entrance of the school tells a lot about the culture and the climate. Keeping the front area clean at all times is important; so is making sure the windows and entrance doors shine. One of the first things the community, parents, and students see is the entrance of the school. The principal needs to think about what he or she wants the community to see and feel when they enter the school. The parents and students always wonder who the teachers and staff members are at each school, so have pictures of the staff in the front entrance. You can group them in a variety of ways—pictures of individuals, a group picture of the entire staff, or pictures of groups according to their grade or content area, such all the first grade teachers or all the social studies teachers. It is very important to have pictures of the entire staff, including custodians, office staff, cooks, and support staff.

Figure 3.3 Office Improvement Planning Template

PLANNING TEMPLATE

General Office Goal: ____________________

Office Areas of Focus: ____________________

Team Members Responsible for Implementing Plan: ____________________

1. General Office Goal Statement	*2. Present Level of Functioning*	*3. Gap Between Present Level of Functioning and Desired Level of Functioning*	*4. Strategies Needed to Be Successful With the Office Goal Area*	*5. Timeline for Implementation*	*6. People Responsible for Strategies or Goal Area*	*7. Vision of What Office Will Look Like if the Goal Is Attained*

SOURCE: Adapted from Eller (2004).

Having pictures of the entire staff gives the front entrance a warm family atmosphere.

Display Case for School Awards and Evidence of Accomplishments

What has the school accomplished? is a question that may be asked by visitors, parents, students, and community members. Set aside an area in the front of the school where staff and students can display their accomplishments and work. Get the staff involved; encourage them to display student work in the cases. This is an area that you want to make sure the custodians clean on a regular basis. Keeping this area neat and clean says a lot about your culture and what is important to you. Parents, visitors, and students always take the time to look at what the school has accomplished.

Staff Lounge

We have been in many staff lounges where the furniture is old and dated. As the principal, you can put a little spice into the lounge without doing all the work yourself. Ask your parent group to get involved! Make sure the lounge is a welcoming place for the staff to have lunch and take a break by providing nice furniture, lamps, couches, a phone, and art work. (This can be students' art work.) Make the lounge a comfortable place for your staff. One way we have maintained the lounge is by giving responsibility for it to a class, the student council, or a group of students who need an extra boost. It is amazing how the students want to help. The students change the bulletin board and keep the lounge decorated and clean. We gave the students permission to put a tip jar in the lounge. The students use the money to purchase things for the lounge, such as lamps and decorations, and occasionally they have treats available for the staff.

Bulletin Board Ideas for Staff

At some schools you may have an area where there is a bulletin board that you could use to display things. This board you can use to welcome staff, students, and families back to school. You can also use the board throughout the year to promote your school, staff, and students.

In the first week of school, have a welcome-back bulletin board for your staff. Get your staff involved in the bulletin board. One idea is to have staff members bring in their baby pictures or pictures of themselves when they were young. Display the pictures on a bulletin board, and then have the staff match the correct baby picture with the right staff member.

Let's say you designate the month of February as "I Love to Read Month." Have the staff bring in their favorite childhood books and short descriptions of why they like the books. Put the books and the descriptions on a display table for the students and staff to see. It is amazing how the students get involved with this activity. It truly inspires the students to read the same book as their teacher.

WELCOMING STAFF BACK TO SCHOOL

ACTIVITY: GETTING TO KNOW YOUR TEACHERS AND STAFF

An important aspect of building a positive school culture and climate is to value your staff. One activity that a principal can do is to meet with every employee before the start of school year. This activity gives the principal the opportunity to get to know the staff and to learn things about the school.

Activity Directions:

• The first step is to send a letter to each employee inviting her or him to meet with you. In the letter, ask the employee to call or e-mail your secretary to set the time and location of the meeting. It is important that the employee selects the location of the meeting. Some staff members may want to meet in their classrooms or offices; some may request that you meet with them at a coffee shop.

• The meetings should be 20 to 30 minutes in length.

• At the meeting it is important to let the employee do most of the talking.

• Be prepared for the meeting by having specific questions you would like to ask each employee. Here are examples of some questions:

1. Tell me a little bit about your personal and professional life.
2. What are some of your dreams and hopes for yourself and the school?
3. What are some positive things about the school?
4. If you could change one thing about the school, what would that be?
5. What are some things you need to be successful in your job?
6. What can I do to make your year successful?

• It is very helpful to take notes during the meeting. Note cards work the best.

• The information you gather about your employees and the school will be beneficial throughout the school year.

Materials/Supplies Needed:

- Note cards and a container for the note cards

After each meeting it is important to review the conversation you had with the employee. It is important to remember key points that the employee shared with you.

ACTIVITY: WELCOME BACK BARBEQUE

A very powerful activity to do with your staff is to have a welcome back barbeque. The event could occur at the school or at a local park. One way to help organize this event is to have your parent group or local businesses help support or fund this event.

Activity Directions:

- Set the date, time, and location.
- Send out invitations to your entire staff.
- Meet with your parent group to ask for support for this event.
- Ask local businesses if they would support the event.
- Once you have the location set and have ordered all the food, decide what will occur at the barbeque. Make sure you have enough grills.
- Offer games or activities for the staff to do, such as badminton, bocce ball, and so forth.
- At the barbeque, introduce new staff members.
- If you do receive donations or support from the community or parent group, be sure to send thank you notes to the donors.

Materials/Supplies Needed:

- Enough food to feed the entire staff
- Grills to cook the food
- Plates, utensils, cups, napkins, and so forth
- Game equipment, such as badminton rackets, bocce ball sets, and so forth

**Other Powerful Activities to Use the
First Week Staff Is Back to Work**

ACTIVITY: REFRESHMENTS FOR STAFF

Meet with the parent group and explain to them how busy the first week back is for the staff. Make a request to the parent group to have food such as bars, cookies, water, and sodas available for the staff the first day they are back to work.

ACTIVITY: BUSINESS CARDS FOR STAFF

You may have noticed almost every business supplies its employees with business cards. One way to begin the year with your staff is to provide them with business cards that they can give to parents and others. This sends a very powerful message to the staff that you value and respect them. Business cards are inexpensive; your parent group may be willing to provide them as a service to your staff. Parents appreciate the cards from their children's teachers. By providing this service, you may reduce the number of phone calls the main office receives from parents requesting to speak to their children's teachers. On the business card it is important to have the teacher's name, school, address, work telephone number, fax number, and e-mail address.

ACTIVITY: NAME PLATES FOR TEACHERS

It is important to create a professional atmosphere and environment at the school. By each classroom door it is important to have the teacher's name on a name plate. The best and most inexpensive kind of name plates are the ones that can change if a teacher changes a room. With this kind of name plate, the plate with the teacher's name slides into a frame that remains attached to the wall next to each door.

ACTIVITY: POSITIVE MESSAGE

Several times a year it is important to leave or write positive message to your staff. Leaving a positive message on a teacher's voice mail is a great way to tell the staff member how important she or he is. To start the year off on a positive note, it is a good idea to leave a message to all staff on the first day of school.

ACTIVITY: FIRST DAY SURVIVAL KIT

A fun way to begin the first day is to give each staff member a survival kit. Some items to put in the kit are listed below:

- Chocolate
- A stress ball

- Life savers
- Aspirin
- A poem or short story about being a teacher
- A yearbook (this gives staff members an opportunity to learn other staff members' and students' names)
- Rubber bands
- A can/bottle of soda
- Apples
- Mints/gum
- Sticky note pads

ACTIVITY: ICE CREAM SOCIAL EVENT

A very easy way to bring people together is to have an ice cream social event. It is very easy to prepare banana splits or ice cream sundaes and this is also a big hit for the staff. It is very important to bring staff together socially without having a meeting. This gives staff a time to visit and share what's happening personally and professionally.

ACTIVITY: BREAKFAST FOR STAFF

Everyone loves a great breakfast. The last couple of years we have had our family help serve breakfast for the staff. It gives the staff time to come together before beginning their day. We usually have music playing in the background when the staff enters the room. This gives staff time to interact with each other and to learn what's happening in their personal and professional lives.

ACTIVITY: WRAPPING UP THE CLASSROOM

Normally, the period leading up to the start of the school year is an exciting time, especially for elementary students. These students can become so excited that they get their parents to bring them to the school to look over their classrooms.

We took advantage of this natural excitement plus helped the teachers get more excited about the upcoming school year by providing teachers with wrapping paper, ribbon, and large bows to use in covering their classroom doors. A PTO representative was asked to connect with each teacher and assist the teacher in decorating the classroom door as if it were a present. On each door we provided a label that said "Do not open until August 21" (the first day of school). This activity built a lot of enthusiasm both among the students and the staff and set a really good tone for the start of the year. It also helped the staff and some of the parents begin to develop a good working relationship. The students were excited to "open their presents" and enter their classrooms for the first time.

STRATEGY: BOOK FAIR GIFTS

A strategy we have found to be fun and helpful in building a positive climate is to use the incentives provided by book fair companies to buy adult-level books for the staff. You normally can get quite a few books from this source. Once you have these books, you can give them to staff members periodically as gifts. When we have given them out, we have selected books that seem to relate to or have some meaning for the staff members receiving them. Then we write little notes in the books, telling the recipients why we think the book is a match for them and thanking them for something they did for the school. Here are some examples:

- A pictorial book on the California coast—We gave this to a teacher who had a daughter living in California.
- A joke book—We gave this to a teacher who always had a joke on the tip of his tongue.
- A travel book for Europe—We gave this book to a teacher who wanted to go to Europe when he retired. We included a travel planner.
- A pasta cookbook—This book was given to a teacher who liked to host dinner parties.

As you can see, this strategy would be very personal and provide your staff members with something useful while letting them know that you know them personally and appreciate the unique qualities they bring to the work setting.

SUMMARY

As you implement the ideas from this chapter, you should begin to see some improvement in the climate of your school. The ideas and strategies contained here are designed to build positive relations and provide a jump start to your school climate and culture improvement efforts. We hope you found activities here that will work for you and help your staff to grow. Keep moving forward on your efforts to improve the climate of your school.

In Chapter 4, Building A Foundation for Your Climate and Culture Improvements, you will learn new ideas and strategies to help you emotionally connect your staff. This is an important attribute of a positive school climate and will lead to a healthy culture. You will see immediate results as you implement some of these ideas.

4

Building an Emotional Base for Your Climate and Culture Improvements

E ducation is a very emotional enterprise. There has been much research done that confirms students remember the emotional aspects of their education (sometimes even more than the academic content). This same can also hold true for adults. The emotional aspects of working in a school are crucial to the success of school climate and culture interventions. A part of the climate involves people's feelings toward actually being at and working at the school. It is important to start your climate and culture improvement efforts by developing a good, sound emotional foundation to build upon.

ABOUT THIS CHAPTER

Ideas and strategies to build a positive emotional foundation are included in this chapter. We will introduce you to emotion-based activities and strategies that will help you to improve the climate and (in turn) the culture of your school. As you review some of the ideas outlined here, keep the following in mind:

- What is the intent of these activities in relation to the improvement of the emotional climate of a school?

- What activities do I see that might work with my staff to help build the necessary emotional connections to begin to change the climate and culture of my school?
- How can these activities and strategies immediately impact the climate of my school and ultimately change its culture?

In this chapter, we have outlined some of the most effective activities we have seen and used in helping staff members to build emotional connections. We know they will work for you in your school.

ACTIVITY: MEASURING THEIR IMPACT

In schools, staff members may not take the time to reflect on how they value each other. Over time, people can take each other for granted, and this will negatively impact the culture of the school. This exercise is designed to help staff members to take the time to reflect on the importance of colleagues and on how they show these colleagues their appreciation for their support.

Activity Directions:

- Explain the importance of collegial relationships in effective schools and the importance of taking the time to understand and improve these relationships.
- Hand out the Measuring Their Impact Activity Sheet (Figure 4.1)
- Ask the staff to think of colleagues who impact them in a personal or professional manner and have them rate the relative importance of these colleagues in their life using the meters provided on the sheet. When they are done, ask them to think about how effectively they communicate the importance/impact each person rated provides to them.
- After people have had time to consider their communication with important colleagues, ask them to respond to the questions at the end of the activity sheet.

Materials/Supplies Needed:

- Activity sheets

ACTIVITY: I REMEMBER WHEN . . .

This activity is designed to help teachers identify the importance of the emotions associated with learning. Many times, participants completing this activity will discover that their most significant memories involve emotions; sometimes negative emotions have played a huge rule in their lives. We want teachers to see that positive emotions are helpful for students' learning.

Figure 4.1 Measuring Their Impact Activity Sheet

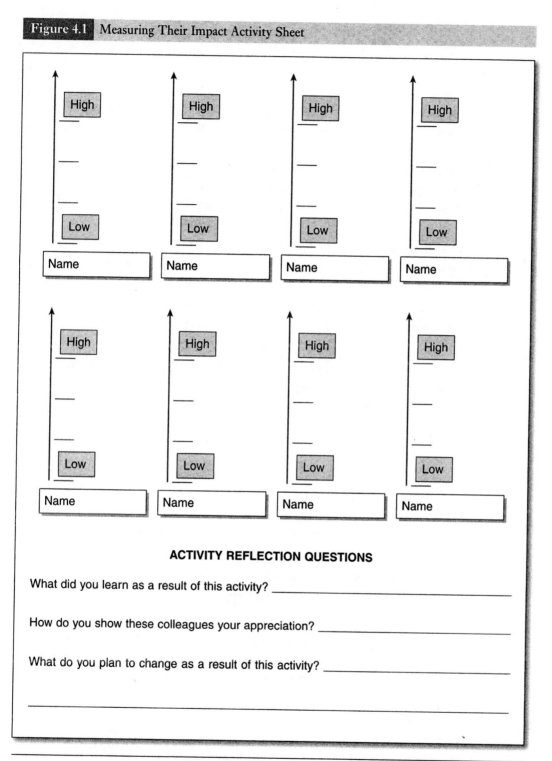

ACTIVITY REFLECTION QUESTIONS

What did you learn as a result of this activity? _____

How do you show these colleagues your appreciation? _____

What do you plan to change as a result of this activity? _____

_____

Activity Directions:

• Hand out the activity sheet for the activity, "I Remember When . . ." (Figure 4.2)

• Ask participants to spend 15 to 20 minutes thinking about their memories of their K–12 educational experience and writing some of the more significant memories on the sheet. The memories listed can be either positive or negative in nature.

• Once most people have completed their sheets, place them in groups of three to four to talk about their experiences. Since some of these experiences may be private in nature, allow individual group members to decide what they should share. Give each group member 5 to 6 minutes to share.

• At the end of the sharing session, ask each group to complete a tally listing the positive and negative emotions identified by their group. This information should be strictly numerical in nature.

• Have each group report out its number. Write the tallies on a large sheet of paper.

• Once the total numbers of positive and negative emotions are listed, ask the groups to meet again for 3 to 4 minutes and talk about their perceptions of the numbers. Once this has been completed, the entire group can discuss their perceptions of the information.

Materials/Supplies Needed:

• Activity sheets for I Remember When . . .

This activity can work well when preparing a group to talk about emotional intelligence, or it can be used during the first few meetings of a group to help them see why their instructional experiences will be designed to be positive.

ACTIVITY: DESCRIPTIVE FOOTWEAR

This activity is designed to pull the staff together around a common theme. It was implemented at one of our schools to provide a common ground around which staff could identify with each other.

Activity Directions:

• Each staff member purchases or brings in a pair of older style canvas shoes. (We used the Chuck Taylor Converse All-Stars.)

• The art teacher or someone else at the school talented in color or design assists faculty members with the process of decorating their shoes,

Figure 4.2   Activity Sheet for I Remember When . . .

I REMEMBER WHEN . . .

School experiences have a profound impact on each of us and our adult lives. Take a few minutes, and write your memories in the boxes corresponding with the major school divisions listed: elementary, middle or junior high, and high school. For each of the divisions, try to list three or four memories that come to mind. Use keywords, short phrases, and abbreviations to help you save time. Also list the dominant emotion that you associate with that memory.

Elementary Years

K	1	2	3	4	5

Middle/Junior High Years

6	7	8

High School Years

9	10	11	12

so each pair has a personal touch. The decorating can take place at a staff meeting. The shoes are decorated with a latex-based paint so that the changes are permanent and flexible and won't fall off when the shoes are handled or worn.

• If some staff are interested in participating in the activity but are unable to be at the decorating session, other staff can paint their shoes.

• At designated times during the year, the staff will all wear their shoes.

• The strategy should be explained to both parents and students.

Materials/Supplies Needed:

• Latex paint
• Shoes as provided by staff

In the school where we first implemented the idea, the parents and the students were interested in looking at the shoes and commented about how the shoes seemed to bring people together.

ACTIVITY: THE BOOT AWARD

The Boot Award is a way of rewarding staff and providing them with an opportunity during the day to visit classrooms, do some research, finish a project, or do anything of their choice. When an employee receives the Boot Award, the principal covers the person's job for a specified period of time. You can provide the employee with as much time as you choose. We have found that covering their job for a period of time from one to two hours is practical and makes the award worthwhile for the employee. The nomination box for the Boot Award can be placed in the lounge or the office so that people have easy access to it.

The objective of the Boot Award is to reward staff members for something positive they did for another employee or for students. Any staff member can nominate someone for the Boot Award. Two sample nomination forms are included in Figure 4.3.

The boot award is an activity designed to involve the staff members in recognizing each other for the good things they do or to compliment other team members for their help and assistance.

Activity Directions:

• The principal secures a boot to use for the Boot Award.

• The principal provides an overview of the procedures for staff nominations for the Boot Award. Some of the key points needed for the overview are as follows:

    o Tell staff that you are starting a new award called the Boot Award. They may nominate a staff member who has done

| Figure 4.3 | Boot Award Nomination Forms |

I nominate _____ for the Boot Award because he or she helped me
with _____.
Signature _____

I nominate _____ for the Boot Award because he or she has been
instrumental in/with _____.
Signature _____

something for them or has shown leadership or dedication at the school.

o Explain to the staff that there is a nomination form that they can complete to nominate a faculty member. Each week, one faculty member's name will be drawn from among the nominations received, and that employee will be given the Boot Award.

o When an employee is awarded the Boot Award, the principal will fill the boot with treats and give the award winner the boot. The winner's name will be announced over the intercom so all the students and staff know who has received the boot award.

• Staff members may nominate each other for the Boot Award based on assistance or support the nominee has provided, extraordinary efforts made by the nominee for student success, or any other positive criteria you establish as a leader or school.

• The staff member keeps the boot for a week and then returns it to the office for the next recipient.

Materials/Supplies Needed:

• A boot to use for holding treats (we use a glass boot we obtained from an "entertainment" institution)
• A nominating box and slips of paper

SOURCE: From *Energizing Staff Meetings* (pp. 120–121), by S. Eller and J. Eller, 2006, Thousand Oaks, CA: Corwin. Copyright 2006 by Corwin. Adapted with permission.

ACTIVITY: JACK-O-LANTERNS

This strategy was used by our colleague Dwayne Young to build an emotional foundation with his staff while also having some fun. Around the Halloween season, he asked grade-level teams to make jack-o-lanterns that illustrated the characteristics of their team, their progress as a team, and so forth. He found that the teams put together some very interesting jack-o-lanterns.

Activity Directions:

- Purchase several small- and medium-sized pumpkins for your staff members. Allow two to three pumpkins per team.

- Share with team members that you want them to make jack-o-lanterns or jack-o-lantern scenes that illustrate something positive about their team, their team characteristics, their team accomplishments, or some other attribute they would like to communicate about their team to others in the building.

- Let them know that they can decorate or carve their pumpkins using markers, paints, or other materials. They can use materials other than the pumpkins to make their scenes or displays, but the pumpkins must make up the majority of the scene.

- Each team should write a half-page description of their pumpkin scene outlining what they were attempting to illustrate in it.

- Once the teams have completed their scenes, the scenes should be brought to the office area for display. The teams should also submit their half-page description.

- Team scenes can be judged based on pre-established criteria, awards may be given, or the scenes can just be enjoyed without judging.

- At a faculty meeting teachers can talk about what they learned about each other as a result of the Jack-O-Lantern activity.

Materials/Supplies Needed:

- An assortment of small- and medium-sized pumpkins
- Markers and paints to decorate the pumpkins
- Various other materials (feathers, sticks, leaves, stickers, construction paper, sequins, etc.) to decorate the pumpkins

SOURCE: Dwayne Young, Centreville Elementary School, Centreville, Virginia. Used with permission.

ACTIVITY: BLOCK OF SUPPORT

One way to build a positive emotional foundation with a school staff is to help them identify the gifts others bring to the school. One approach to this is the activity described below, in which each staff member is issued a permanent marker and a two-inch wooden cube. Staff members write positive attributes or compliments about each staff member on his or her block, thus helping each person see how valued he or she is by the school and other staff members.

Activity Directions:

- Provide each staff member with a two-inch wooden cube and a permanent marker.

- Have each staff member write his or her name on the block and pass the block to another staff member.

- The person receiving the block writes a positive word or phrase (related to the owner of the block) on the block.

- Continue passing the blocks around the room until all sides of the blocks are filled. If some staff members are not at the meeting during this activity, make sure to pass around blocks for them.

- After the blocks have been passed around the room, the owners get them back. Each person now has a block with at least six positive comments on it.

Materials/Supplies Needed:

- A two-inch wooden cube for each person on the staff
- Permanent markers

In our experience in using this strategy, teachers have kept their blocks in prominent spots on their desks for years after they have received them. At times, we have even asked people to bring their blocks to a meeting to remind them of the activity. Some teachers have even used this idea in their classrooms with students.

SOURCE: From *Energizing Staff Meetings* (p. 108), by S. Eller and J. Eller, 2006, Thousand Oaks, CA: Corwin. Copyright 2006 by Corwin. Adapted with permission.

ACTIVITY: ARTIFACT INTRODUCTIONS

This activity is designed to help group members get to know a lot about each other in a short period of time. It also helps a group to build deep and meaningful relationships that will be key to the operation of the organization. We have used this activity with both new and existing groups with great success. We have found that even though members of an existing group may be familiar with each other, in many cases they truly don't "know" each other. We have found this activity to be especially helpful in setting a positive emotional foundation for school climate and culture improvement projects.

Activity Directions:

• Ask participants to bring an item or artifact to a group meeting that represents them either personally or professionally. Let them know they will each have an opportunity to take one minute to share the artifact and tell how it represents them with the entire group.

• At the group meeting, remind individuals of the parameters of the activity; each person will share their artifact for 1 or 2 minutes and talk about how the artifact describes him or her in a personal or professional manner.

• Be sure they understand the purpose of doing the activity: to get to know each other in a deeper manner so they can connect with and help each other in the future.

• Have the entire group sit in a circle facing each other. As the leader or facilitator, you should share your artifact first, modeling the process for others.

• For a group consisting of approximately 20 members, the activity usually lasts about 40 minutes. For larger groups the activity may last over an hour. In these larger groups, it is a good idea to hold the artifact sharing over two separate sessions.

• About halfway through a session, it is a good idea to stop the activity, allow people a chance to stand and stretch, and then have them talk with a partner about what they're learning about each other as result of the activity. Once the activity has been completed, be sure to debrief it by asking group members to talk about what they have learned as a result of hearing other people's artifact introductions.

Materials/Supplies Needed:

• None

ACTIVITY: THE THANK YOU BLITZ

In many cases, staff members go a long time between receiving thank you notes from others. This lack of appreciation can become part of the school culture and lead to negative staff relations. The Thank You Blitz is an activity that can increase appreciation and turn the tide on a negative climate and culture.

Activity Directions:

- The meeting leader talks to the staff about the importance of appreciation and recognition.
- Each staff member is provided with a packet of 25 thank you notes. (These notes can be provided by the school parent group, ordered through bulk supply houses, or made on the computer and duplicated at the school.)
- Each staff member is given a thank you log (Figure 4.4). On the log are columns for the days of the week, the people the notes are sent to, and the reason for the notes being sent. Staff members are asked to take part in the activity for one month, keeping track of the thank you notes they send out on the thank you note log.
- At the end of the month, staff members are asked to reflect on their thank you logs privately and then talk about the process at a staff meeting.
- This activity is designed to change the climate of the school in the short term, but it works to positively impact the culture of the school in relation to the appreciation the staff members show each other for their hard work.

Materials/Supplies Needed:

- Thank you notes
- Thank You Blitz logs

ACTIVITY: CANDLE CEREMONY

During the course of the year, many life- or career-changing events happen. When we are getting ready to close down a significant project or the entire school year, sometimes it's easy to just take care of the business-related aspects and forget about the emotional aspects. The candle ceremony is an activity we have used with various groups over the years to help them as they move out of an emotional project or close down the school year.

Activity Directions:

- In a room that you are able to darken, set up a large candle in the middle of a table surrounded by smaller candles. Arrange the smaller candles randomly around the larger candle.
- Place chairs around the candle table in a circular manner. The placement works best if the person in each chair will have access to the candle table without having to walk around or between other people.

Figure 4.4   The Thank You Blitz Log

THE THANK YOU BLITZ LOG

Use this log to keep track of the thank you notes you distribute for the next month. At the end of the month, reflect on what you have done in relation to your colleagues and what you have received in return. Be ready to talk about the Thank You Blitz at a future staff meeting.

Day of the Week	Person Receiving Note/Date	Reason for Note
Monday		
Tuesday		
Wednesday		
Thursday		
Friday		
Saturday		
Sunday		

- Light the larger candle in the middle of the table, but leave the smaller candles unlit.

- Darken the room by turning off the lights and pulling the curtains or shades. The room does not have to be very dark, but the majority of light in the room should come from the candle.

- Ask teachers to come to the candle room and find a seat.

- Explain the directions for the activity. Here is an example of what you could say:
  - "As a way to close down [this project] [the school year], I want to give you a chance to thank your colleagues who helped you to be successful.
  - "As you can see, a candle is lit in the center of the table. This candle represents the collective energy and passion we hold for success as a staff.
  - "In a minute, I am going to give you a chance to come up and light a candle and then talk for about 30 seconds to thank someone who helped you be successful or work through a difficult situation during [this school year] [this complex project].
  - "Once you have lit your candle, you can set it on the table, and another person will be able to come up and do the same thing. We will continue the activity until everyone has had an opportunity to participate and thank a colleague."

- One at a time, teachers come up to the candle table, light a small candle from the flame of the large candle, and thank someone (either in the room or not) for something specific that person did to help the person lighting the candle get through or survive the school year (or the project).

- Once the person lighting the candle and thanking the other person has finished speaking, another person comes up to do the same two tasks. Allow people to come up randomly to light their candles and thank their colleagues.

- Once everyone has had a chance to light a candle, allow the group a moment of silence to contemplate their ceremony.

- Once the moment of silence is over, spend a minute or two and talk about the following:
  - "We've had a [productive year] [successful project] and helped each other be successful.
  - "The candle in the middle of the table represents our school and our collective collegial relationships.
  - "Now that the [school year] [project] is over, we will all need to go off on our own for a while. Your individual candle represents the strength of the group transferred to each of you (by the flame of the large candle being transferred to your individual candle).

   o "As you work to continue your positive impact on others outside
      of the school, take the energy of the group here with you. The
      [school year] [project] is officially closed. Stay safe, make a posi-
      tive contribution to others, and [come back] [continue to be] ready
      to make a difference in the lives of your students.
   o "Please feel free to take a candle with you as a reminder of this
      ceremony and the collective strength of us as a staff."

- After your closing talk, blow out the main candle in the middle of
the table and allow each person to take a smaller candle home as a souvenir
of the ceremony.

Materials/Supplies Needed:

- A large (3-inch diameter, 6-inch tall) candle
- Enough small (1½-inch diameter, 2-inch tall) candles for each person
  at the meeting
- A small table
- A table cover (to protect the table from wax drippings)
- Enough chairs for the entire staff

ACTIVITY: BAG OF POSITIVE PHRASES

The Bag of Positive Phrases is an activity that is fun and helps to build
emotional connections among the staff.

Activity Directions:

- The activity normally takes place at a staff meeting. At the beginning
of the meeting, give each staff member a bag or paper sack.

- Have the staff members decorate their bags and put their names on
their bags.

- Place the bags at locations around the room.

- Provide each person at the meeting with some sticky notes or other
note paper, and have the staff members write positive notes to one another.
Have them place the notes in the bags for each staff member spread
around the room. The staff members can sign their names to the notes, or
the notes can be anonymous.

- After 5 to 10 minutes, stop the writing part of the activity, and have
the owners of the bags or sacks go and pick them up. Give them a minute
or two to read the notes they have received.

- Ask staff members to think about what they learned as they wrote
the notes and as they read the notes that others wrote about them.

Materials/Supplies Needed:

- Paper bags
- Markers
- Note paper and pencils

This is a rewarding activity for the staff to do. It is exciting to watch the staff read their notes. This activity would be fun to do during the month of February, when people can get bogged down and need something to lift their spirits. If you don't have time during a faculty meeting to do the activity, you can place the bags around the room in the faculty lounge, and give people a set amount of time to write their notes. The "full" bags can be brought to a faculty meeting or placed in faculty members' mail boxes. It is important to include all staff members, including cooks, custodians, office staff, teachers, and paraprofessionals in this activity. Even though it is a simple idea, it builds a strong positive atmosphere in a school faculty. We have seen staff members who have kept their Bags of Positives close to their desks or work stations for a number of years after completing the activity.

SOURCE: From *Energizing Staff Meetings* (pp. 108–109), by S. Eller and J. Eller, 2006, Thousand Oaks, CA: Corwin. Copyright 2006 by Corwin. Adapted with permission.

ACTIVITY: SPREAD THE WORD

Spread the Word is an activity designed to help the staff identify positive attributes about the school or each other.

Activity Directions:

- On a long table or a large wall surface, spread out a piece of plain cloth or paper, and tell staff members that you will give them 5 to 10 minutes to write down as many positive comments as they can think of about each other on the paper or cloth.

- Ask each staff member to write down a certain number of comments or to write comments about certain people (to make sure there is at least one positive comment on the chart about each person).

- As you lead the activity, be sure to look at the chart or cloth as people are writing to make sure that everyone is receiving a positive comment. If you notice that someone is not getting comments, stop and write something down for that person.

- Once a large number of comments have been written down, display the completed chart or sheet in the lounge or in a place where the staff gathers.

- At follow-up staff meetings, ask people what they learned about the activity and how they think it helped them as a staff to connect and work together. Also, ask people how this activity could be helpful in their work with students.

Materials/Supplies Needed:

- Markers
- Plain bed sheet, tablecloth, or large piece of paper

This is another activity that works well as a posted object in the staff lounge over a set period of time. This gives people a chance to think and write down lots of comments. Use several sheets divided by grade levels or departments if you are working with a large faculty.

SOURCE: From *Energizing Staff Meetings* (pp. 109–110), by S. Eller and J. Eller, 2006, Thousand Oaks, CA: Corwin. Copyright 2006 by Corwin. Adapted with permission.

STRATEGY: REWARD WITH A SMILE

Another way of providing staff with a positive reinforcement is to fill a container with treats, such as M&M's candy, jelly beans, candy bars, and so forth and give it to a staff member. (For example, we were able to find a container that had a smiley face on the lid, and we gave it to a staff member along with a positive note explaining why she was receiving the treat). The staff member who receives the container eats the candy, enjoys the note, and then repeats the process: He or she fills the container with candy, adds a positive note, and passes it on to another staff member. This strategy helps to build a positive foundation for future climate and culture initiatives, because it builds personal relationships. The person receiving the note normally doesn't expect it; the surprise helps to build positive relationships among the staff. We have seen people look in their mail boxes and let out a loud "all right" when they pull out the candy box. The excitement for this strategy goes far beyond the food value of the candy; it relates to the fact that someone on the staff cared enough about an individual to write a note, fill the container, and pass it on.

This strategy works well when there are several containers circulating among the faculty at once. It has worked well for us in the past when we started several candy containers at the same time and placed time guidelines on their "passing." Normally, it works well to have the containers change "locations" about once a week. You can remind staff members to pass their containers in the weekly bulletin or through some other method. We have tried to watch the process to make sure that the containers kept moving and have had to add more containers to the group when we noticed that there were holdups in the process.

Be sure to talk about the strategy in staff meetings to get people's perceptions of what they are gaining as a result of passing the containers. After a period of time (maybe a month or two), it is a good idea to call in the containers and give people a break from the activity. You want to do this to keep the activity from becoming stale and overused. In future container passings, you may want to vary the rewards such as including coupons, sticker pages, or other items that people would like to get. Be sure to involve everyone on your staff, including custodians, cooks, paraprofessionals, secretaries, the principal, and others that can benefit from getting positive notes about their performance or personality at school.

SOURCE: From *Energizing Staff Meetings* (pp. 110–111), by S. Eller and J. Eller, 2006, Thousand Oaks, CA: Corwin. Copyright 2006 by Corwin. Adapted with permission.

ACTIVITY: A NOVEL STAFF

This activity can be fun and helps people to connect in a positive manner. It involves having the group compile a book about the staff.

Activity Directions:

• Designate a page of a blank book for each staff member; write a staff member's name on each page. Pass the book around the staff, and ask people to write positive comments, stories, or other interesting anecdotes about the person. Provide enough time for people to think and fill in the book. It may take several staff meetings or a couple of weeks with the book in the staff lounge to accomplish this.

• Once the book is completed, place it where the staff members have access to it and can look it at from time to time.

Materials/Supplies Needed:

• A blank book (these are the books that schools purchase that contain only blank pages allowing children to publish their own books)

A Novel Staff has several variations that you might consider to make it even more engaging for your staff. Here are some to consider:

• Ask staff members to make their page more personal by writing some basic information about themselves, such as their background, educational philosophy, their thoughts about teaching, and so forth. This helps others to learn something about each staff member as they are writing their positives about each person.

- Have each staff member put together a collage or drawing that illustrates himself or herself as a person and a professional. This illustration can be created on another paper and pasted into the book.

- Ask staff members to select their favorite poem, phrase, or quotation to include as an example of their beliefs to include on their page in the book. Those writing in the book will learn something about the person to help them as they develop their compliments or positive ideas.

- Have team members or colleagues select illustrations, poems, quotations, or other writings to include on each person's page as examples of what each person represents as a person and a professional. This will also help individuals reading their pages learn what others think.

SOURCE: From *Energizing Staff Meetings* (pp. 111–112), by S. Eller and J. Eller, 2006, Thousand Oaks, CA: Corwin. Copyright 2006 by Corwin. Adapted with permission.

ACTIVITY: FLOATING OR TRAVELING TROPHY

People like rewards and ceremonies. We have found the idea of giving traveling trophies both fun and a good way to build a positive climate in a school.

Activity Directions:

- Decide on the criteria or categories for a floating or traveling trophy. Here are some you might consider:
  - For the staff member who did or said the funniest or most humorous thing at school
  - For the person who made the biggest funny mistake
  - For the teacher who turned around a difficult student
  - For the person who helped out other staff members with a problem
  - For the teacher who had the most interesting parent–teacher conference story
  - For any other reason that would be entertaining or meaningful for staff

- Once you have decided on the criteria for the traveling trophy, select the time frame. You can award traveling trophies for long (the entire school year) or short (monthly) periods of time. Decide on the time frame that is appropriate and most meaningful for your staff members.

- Provide an overview of the criteria for the trophy. Explain the process for staff nominations for the trophy. Use a nomination form to allow staff to nominate a colleague for the trophy.

Materials/Supplies Needed:

- An object to use for the traveling trophy. You might find an old trophy and put your own label or title on it. You can use a statue in place of a trophy, such as a flamingo, cow, lion, or some other interesting figurine.

This simple idea has become meaningful for staff members over the years. People look forward to the presentation of these trophies and have nominated others for both funny and meaningful awards. The traveling nature of these trophies is very motivational for people and builds a positive culture in the school.

SOURCE: From *Energizing Staff Meetings* (pp. 112–113), by S. Eller and J. Eller, 2006, Thousand Oaks, CA: Corwin. Copyright 2006 by Corwin. Adapted with permission.

ACTIVITY: JELLY BEAN QUESTIONS

The Jelly Bean Questions activity helps team members communicate and get to know more about each other in a structured way. It can be used for small groups or for groups that are larger.

Activity Directions:

- Give each participant a clear plastic bag with an assortment of colored jelly beans inside. Also give each a sheet that contains questions that are color-coded to the jelly beans in the bag.
- Ask participants, one at a time, to choose one jelly bean from their bag and answer the question that corresponds to the color of that bean.
- Go around the group or table until everyone has had a chance to answer one question.
- Once an initial question has been answered, engage the team in a second round. Either let team members select their own bean color, or draw one each round at random.
- After several rounds, engage group members in a brief discussion about what they learned about each other as a result of the activity.

Materials/Supplies Needed:

- An assortment of jelly beans that includes four to six different colors. There should be enough beans so that every group member has two to three of each color in their plastic bag.
- Small, clear sandwich bags in which to place the beans.
- A list of questions corresponding to the various bean colors. An example is included in Figure 4.5.

Figure 4.5 Jelly Bean Question Sheet

JELLY BEAN QUESTIONS

In this activity, you will be asked to draw one jelly bean from your bag and then answer a question that corresponds to the color of the jelly bean you draw. This activity is designed to help members of your group get to know more about each other.

Questions:

- Red—Name a famous person from history you would like to meet.
- Red—What do you think the greatest need of the world is? How would you go about fulfilling this need if you were a world leader?

- Yellow—What is your favorite author's name? Give an example of a book by this author.
- Yellow—Share an example of a difficult problem you have solved lately. How did you go about designing and implementing a solution?

- Blue—If you had one wish, what would be?
- Blue—What would you like to do if you had one week off work and no budget limits?

- Green—Share a meaningful story or event that happened to you while you were in school.
- Green—What hobbies do you like to pursue outside of work?

- Purple—Share a meaningful story or event that happened while you were teaching children.
- Purple—What do you think are the three greatest problems facing our profession?

As you think about implementing this activity with your group, be sure to generate questions that will help the members to get to know more about each other. The more they know and understand, the better they will function together as a team.

ACTIVITY: SNOWBALL FIGHT

The snowball fight activity can be an energizing and emotional building experience for your staff members. It also helps people get to know each other in a deeper and more meaningful way than they normally do in a staff setting.

Activity Directions:

- Give each teacher a blank sheet of paper.

- Give each teacher the following directions about what to write on the paper:
    - Share something about yourself that nobody in the room knows.
    - If you could have one wish come true, what would it be?
    - Share a significant moment that touched your life as a teacher.
    - Draw a rough picture of a place that makes you feel happy and relaxed.

- Divide the group into two equal groups, and have them stand in two single-file lines facing each other.

- Tell group members to crumple their papers into a paper wad or snowball.

- At your signal, the groups throw their paper wads at each other as if they were having a snowball fight.

- Group members pick up the "snowballs" that land by them and throw them at others; they continue to keep the fight going until you call time.

- Have each person pick up a paper wad, unravel it, and try to find the person to whom it belongs. Once they locate that person, they engage in conversation about the information on the paper. This part of the process can be a little chaotic as people try to find the "owners" of the paper wads, but it usually works itself out in a few minutes.

- Have team members continue to move around the room until all of the paper owners are located and have had discussions. This may take several pairings.

- Once all the owners have been identified, engage the entire group in a conversation. You may have the group discuss questions such as the following:
    - What did you learn from this activity?
    - How do you feel that learning more about each other will help us as we work together in the future?
    - What clues did you use to find the person who owned your snowball?
    - How might this activity be used in a classroom?

Materials/Supplies Needed:

- Blank sheets of paper
- Pencils or pens

SOURCE: From *Energizing Staff Meetings* (pp. 113–114), by S. Eller and J. Eller, 2006, Thousand Oaks, CA: Corwin. Copyright 2006 by Corwin. Adapted with permission.

SUMMARY

Building a sound emotional foundation at the start of your school climate and culture improvement project is crucial. Developing connections between teachers is important for principals who are trying to improve the climate and ultimately the culture of their schools. If teachers can feel that they know their colleagues and have a sense of connection with them, a more cooperative spirit is developed. This cooperative spirit transfers to improve the climate of the school and over time becomes an integral part of the culture of the school. People learn to work better together and pull together in order to work through the problems and issues they face.

In Chapter 5, Staff Meeting Starters to Build Culture, you will learn about ideas and strategies that naturally fit into segments of regular staff meetings. These short but sweet activities help to develop a positive climate at schools and also work to improve the culture over time. Even though they are short in nature, we have found them especially helpful to use with staff members. As you begin to integrate activities into your regular meetings, you will see more energized meetings and a positive climate develop over time.

5

Staff Meeting Starters to Build Culture

In many cases, teachers have a hard time in staff meetings. Staff meetings should be a time for people to get together and learn from each other. Also, staff meetings should be opportunities for people to learn more about each other and how to work together in a more productive fashion. In schools where the culture is negative, staff meetings can be a big waste of time. Principals working to improve the school culture use their staff meetings in a productive manner to impact the learning of staff members. Great staff meetings need great starting activities to make them productive.

ABOUT THIS CHAPTER

In this chapter, you will learn about ideas to start staff meetings that work to improve the climate and culture of your school.

As you review the contents of this chapter, look for the following:

- What kinds of activities are helpful in building a positive climate and culture related to starting staff meetings?
- What is it important for all staff to see and hear the growth we are making to improve our school climate and culture?

ACTIVITY: GOOD NEWS

The Good News activity is powerful, because it starts out a faculty meeting on a positive note. Once the positive tone has been set, the rest of the meeting is set to be positive. We have used the activity with all levels of staff with great success.

Activity Directions:

- On the agenda for the staff meeting, the item "Good News" is listed, and about 10 minutes are provided for the item to be shared and discussed.

- At the start of the meeting, talk about the importance of the school climate and culture and why "Good News" is being placed on the meeting agenda.

- Once the rationale is shared, ask staff members to share a positive event from either their personal or professional lives. (Normally we have talked with a few staff members in advance of the meeting and asked them to prepare a Good News item. This helps us to avoid the silence while we are waiting for people to share.)

- As each staff member shares, others at the meeting listen. No comments or judgments are made.

- Once the activity is over (either time has run out, or Good News items have run out) ask staff members to meet in small teams of two to three people and talk about what they have learned as a result of the process.

- After the small groups have finished their discussions, open the discussion to the large group. People should talk about what they have learned about each other or the group as a result of the activity.

Materials/Supplies Needed:

- None

In the initial stages of discussion, the ideas may come out slowly, but once people get accustomed to the process of Good News, ideas and items will come more quickly.

ACTIVITY: HUMAN BINGO

Activity Directions:

- At the start of the meeting, each person is given a card that is laid out like a bingo card (see Figure 5.1; use Figure 5.2 as a template to create your own).

- Within each square of the bingo card, there is a question or statement that describes a person on the team. All of the cards ask for identical information from participants.

- Once all staff members have a card, they are asked to find people who fit into the categories on the card.

- When a person is found who satisfies the category listed in the square on the card, that person's name is written in the square, and an X is placed in the square. That square is considered filled.

- Like the game of bingo, people try to fill their cards in rows, diagonals, or other preestablished patterns.

The first person who fills the bingo card calls out "Bingo!" and wins the activity.

Materials/Supplies Needed:

- Human Bingo Card similar to that shown in Figure 5.1

After playing the game, ask staff these questions:

- What did you learn about each other as a result of the activity?
- How do you think we can use what we learned as we work together?
- What were some of your favorite categories and answers?

SOURCE: From *Energizing Staff Meetings* (pp. 49–51), by S. Eller and J. Eller, 2006, Thousand Oaks, CA: Corwin. Copyright 2006 by Corwin. Adapted with permission.

ACTIVITY: WHO'S CONNECTED?

at risk kids?

We've seen this activity implemented in a variety of settings, but we've never seen a name listed for it. It seems to work best in large, secondary schools where it's easy for students to slip through the cracks and be neglected. We've included it here in this section because of the graphic way that it identifies the students who do not get any attention. It is good in a staff meeting, because it stimulates so much conversation and focus on the part of the staff members.

Activity Directions:

- Conduct the activity in a large room such as the library, gym, or cafeteria to allow staff members to move freely around the room.

- In advance of the meeting, make a Connection Sheet for each student similar to the one shown in Figure 5.3. (The pictures of the students can be obtained through the school's photography company.)

Figure 5.1 Human Bingo Example Sheet

HUMAN BINGO

Find a person who has more than four grandchildren. Name____	Identify someone who has worked overseas. Name____	Find the person who has the most interesting story about an influential person in his or her life. Name____	Find a person who is enrolled in a graduate program. Name____	Locate the person who has the largest junk collection. Name____
Who has recently built a new home? Name____	What person was born the farthest distance from this location? Name____	Find the person who has lived in the most houses in his or her lifetime? Name____	Which person here has the most children? Name____	Locate a person who has had an interesting summer or part-time job. Name____
What person has traveled the most outside of the United States? Name____	Find the person with an interesting story about working with others in a conflict mode. Name____	Free Space	Find someone with an unusual hobby. Name____	Find someone with a funny child-related story. Name____
Find someone with a warmhearted child-related story. Name____	Who has eaten the most unusual food? Name____	Which staff members were born closest to this school? Name____	Who drove the farthest distance from home during last summer's vacation? Name____	Find the person who has met the most famous celebrity. Name____
Find the person who has had the most different jobs over the years. Name____	Who has experienced the most unusual vacation? Name____	Find someone who has an unusual zoo story. Name____	Identify the person with the most pets. Name____	Locate the person who has traveled to a higher point on earth than anyone else. Name____

HUMAN BINGO

Name____	Name____	Name____	Name____	Name____
Name____	Name____	Name____	Name____	Name____
Name____	Name____	Free Space	Name____	Name____
Name____	Name____	Name____	Name____	Name____
Name____	Name____	Name____	Name____	Name____

SOURCE: Eller & Eller (2006). Adapted from the work of Robert Garmston and Bruce Wellman.

Figure 5.3   Connection Sheet

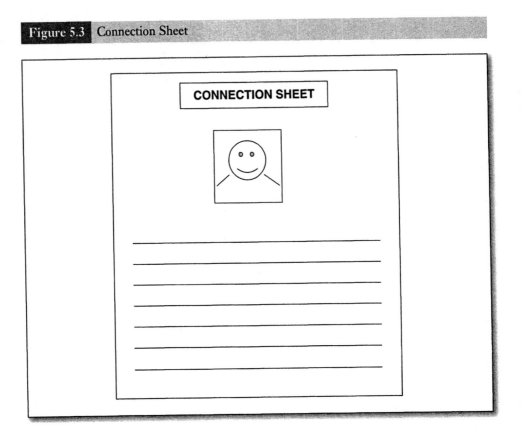

- Post the Connection Sheets around the room. They can be posted randomly, or by grade level, by gender, or in whatever way makes the most sense for the faculty.

- Give each staff member a pencil or pen, and ask them to travel around the room and look at the Connection Sheets. Tell them to write their names on each Connection Sheet for a student with whom they have a significant connection or relationship. (You can develop a local definition for a significant connection or relationship, but we have used criteria such as "talk to the student at least twice a week," "know the student by name," and "know one or two significant facts about the student." In some schools we have even had to set the criteria based on just knowing the student's name.)

- The time for this activity can vary, but we have seen it done in 15 to 20 minutes in some schools, while in others it took a whole hour.

- At the end of the allotted time, ask staff members to examine the Connection Sheets to see what trends emerge. Normally staff members find there are several students who have no teacher names listed on their Connection Sheets, some students who have a few names listed, and others who have lots of names listed.

- Once the staff has identified the trends, ask them what they want to do about the trends. This question usually evokes some kind of response related to a plan to connect with the students who have few or no names listed on their Connection Sheets. In some schools, the staff set a goal themselves to connect with these students; in other schools, the principal has assigned staff members to certain unconnected students.

- Staff members can then develop a goal to connect with the unconnected students as a part of the school improvement planning process, as a team goal, as a goal related to their teacher evaluation process, and so forth.

- Take the Connection Sheets down at the end of the activity to ensure that students will not see them. At a follow-up meeting later in the year, post the Connection Sheets and ask the teachers to either repeat the activity or provide an update on their progress to connect with the students.

- You can also ask the teachers to share what they learned about themselves, the school, and the culture of the school as a result of the activity.

Materials/Supplies Needed:

- Connection Sheets for all students

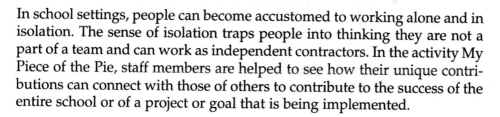

ACTIVITY: MY PIECE OF THE PIE

In school settings, people can become accustomed to working alone and in isolation. The sense of isolation traps people into thinking they are not a part of a team and can work as independent contractors. In the activity My Piece of the Pie, staff members are helped to see how their unique contributions can connect with those of others to contribute to the success of the entire school or of a project or goal that is being implemented.

Activity Directions:

- Explain that in order for the school (or project) to be successful, a team effort is required. An important aspect of a team is that people with diverse backgrounds and experiences connect together to form a group that is stronger than the sum of the parts that are connected. Explain that the exercise My Piece of the Pie will help the group identify those crucial contributions and connections.

- Cut a large round cardboard disc (similar to the kind that comes with frozen pizza) into pieces (like pizza pieces). Divide it into enough "slices" so that everyone on the staff or team has a slice. (Larger groups require larger cardboard discs to ensure the individual slices and big enough to decorate and be seen by other group members.)

- Give each group member one of the slices; provide markers, pens, paints, and other decoration supplies; and ask group members to decorate their pieces to reflect their personalities. Ask them also to write words or phrases that denote how they positively contribute to the project or school and its success. Give members about 5 to 10 minutes to decorate their slices.

- Once all of the slices are decorated, ask group members to tell how their slices represent them and how they contribute to the success of the school or project.

- Post slices as they are shared, and arrange them back in the original disc or pizza shape.

- After completing this activity, ask team members to meet in small groups of three or four and talk about what they have learned about each other and the project as a result of this activity. Have teams report out on their learning to the larger group.

Materials/Supplies Needed:

- Cardboard discs
- Scissors
- Markers, pens, paints, and other decoration supplies

ACTIVITY: I'M A CARD

This activity is designed to help mix a group plus give them a way to get to know each other on a deeper level.

Activity Directions:

- In preparation for the meeting, set up tables are for groups of five or six staff members.

- Place a plant in the middle of each table with a stick holding a large playing card inserted in the base of the plant. (These cards are available at training supply companies, or they can be made by enlarging photocopies of playing cards and pasting them on cardboard). One card (for example, an ace of spades, a five of hearts, etc.) is placed at each table.

- As they enter the staff meeting, ask each staff member to randomly choose a card from a deck (or two decks for a larger faculty group).

- Ask staff members to sit at the table that corresponds to the card he or she has picked.

- Once all staff members have been seated, give the following directions:
  - o At each of the tables we should have groups that are randomly mixed and cover a variety of roles at the school. (For example, you may have teachers, cooks, custodians, etc., sitting at each table).
  - o Once we start the activity, the members of each group, in turn, should spend about 1 to 3 minutes sharing their names and the roles they serve at the school as well as an attribute of the card and how it relates to each of them personally or professionally. (You can share some possible examples, such as "Our card has a five on it, and I have five grandchildren," or "Our card is the queen of hearts, I have a big heart for animals," or "Our card bends but won't break. I am flexible but I have a bottom line.")

- Once all of the group members have shared their ideas, ask the group to share two or three of the ideas with the larger group.

- Ask the entire group to share what they learned about each other as a result of the activity and how they will use what they learned in the future.

- Have each small group determine the best example shared at their table. The plant used to hold up the card sign can be given to the person who shared the best example at each table.

Materials/Supplies Needed:

- Plant for each table
- Enlarged playing cards
- One or two decks of playing cards

SUMMARY

Staff meetings provide a perfect opportunity to improve the climate of your school. When climate-improving activities become a part of your staff meetings, they help to build a culture where staff members come to expect good staff meetings and meaningful activities. Good staff meetings become part of the culture of the school. The activities presented in this chapter can help you as you work to improve the climate and culture of your school.

6

Activities to Couple With Tasks and Decisions

I t's important for you as a school principal working to improve school culture to make sure you include activities that help your staff members accomplish important tasks while also increasing their abilities to work together in a collaborative manner. By doing this you can help them improve their skills while getting needed tasks completed.

ABOUT THIS CHAPTER

This chapter will focus on activities and strategies that can be used when you have to complete tasks. As you read this chapter look for the following:

- How do the strategies presented allow staff members to learn collaboration while also getting important work completed?
- What strategies would work with the particular processing styles of my staff members?
- What strategies do I feel comfortable implementing based on my leadership style?

In this chapter, we have provided a wide variety of activities and strategies that have been proven with staff in a wide range of educational settings—elementary, middle, and high school as well as at the college level. Select and try those that you think will match the needs and strengths of your group.

ACTIVITY: FUTURE SET

A *future set* commonly references current, possible, and preferred states. It is a planning tool for establishing a mental set through reflection about where programs, individuals, or groups are and want to be. This practice involves emotional tension and judgment about matters of great motivational consequence to participants. It is normally conducted in small groups at tables supplied with paper and marking materials. The activity helps to improve school climate and culture, because it actively involves participants in envisioning the future.

Activity Directions:

- Divide participants into workgroups of three to six; randomly select group members to provide for a variety of ideas.
- Ask each group to select a facilitator to manage participation, procedures, time, and recording of information.
- Provide a Future Set planning sheet for each group. A sample of this planning sheet is shown in Figure 6.1.
- Identify the subject or topic of the activity.
- Beginning with the present state, have subgroups brainstorm and record the present state of the subject or topic.
- Proceed to the worst-case scenario; have the subgroups discuss and record the future characteristics of the subject if everything that could go wrong did go wrong.
- Have the subgroups then turn their attention to the preferred future and forecast the desirable attributes that would describe the subject if everything that could go well did go well.
- As a whole group, discuss the activity, first focusing on the present state, then the worst case, and finally the preferred future.
- Ask the group to prioritize the ideas and strategies that will lead the project to the preferred future and keep it out of the worst-case situation.

Materials/Supplies Needed:

- Future Set planning sheets
- Pens, pencils, markers

Figure 6.1 Future Set Planning Sheet

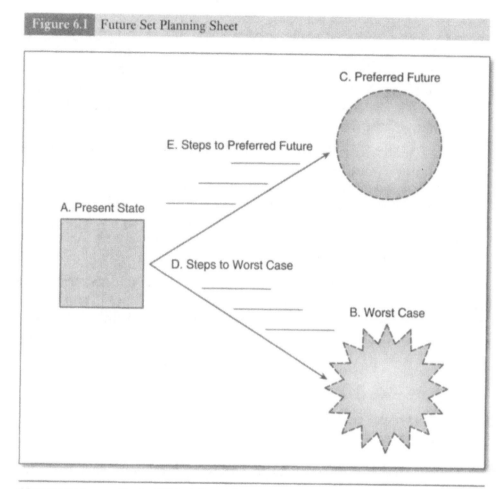

C. Preferred Future

E. Steps to Preferred Future

A. Present State

D. Steps to Worst Case

B. Worst Case

SOURCE: Dickmann, Stanford-Blair, & Rosati-Bojar (2004).

ACTIVITY: CAROUSELING

A highly effective and energizing activity involves carouseling to generate information. In carouseling, the leader gets maximum participation from the people at the meeting.

Activity Directions:

- Divide a large group into smaller teams of four to six people.

- Assign each team a task that must be completed within 8 to 10 minutes; the results of their work should be written on chart paper that is stationed at various locations throughout the room, one chart for each team.

- At the end of the work time, direct each team to designate about half of the team as "travelers" and the other half as "stayers."

- Tell the group that the team members designated as travelers will move to other teams during the activity; those designated as stayers will stay at their charts. The stayers' job is to explain their team's work and ideas to the travelers from other teams who will visit their chart later in the activity. Travelers will visit the other teams' charts to listen to those stayers explain the work done by their teams and to offer suggestions for clarification or improvement.

- Next, ask the travelers to take a marker and move to the chart that is located in a clockwise position from their original chart. Once they are at the new chart, they need to listen to the explanation of the work provided by the stayers there; then they should provide at least two ideas that either clarify or improve the work outlined on the chart before them. They can write their ideas directly on the chart they are visiting with the marker they have brought with them.

- After 3 to 5 minutes, signal the travelers to move to the next chart (see Figure 6.2). Have the travelers rotate three or four times to new charts, and then ask them to return to their original teams. At this point, those who traveled and those who stayed talk about what they learned during this process.

Materials/Supplies Needed:

- Chart paper posted on walls
- Pens, pencils, markers

Carouseling can be used for a variety of purposes. Here are some examples:

- Brainstorming ideas from common topic areas
- Brainstorming ideas from a variety of topic areas
- Generating a pro/con list
- Clarifying topics
- Generating questions
- Generating answers to questions
- Helping a group to simplify a complex topical area

Here's a specific example of how we used carouseling recently with a group. We worked with a school staff to help them better understand the details of their school improvement plan. The plan had been developed by a school improvement team. At the beginning of the session, we pulled out the major strategies to be implemented that were outlined in the plan. These strategies included adjusting the school's schedule to provide a study period to help students who required additional learning support, implementing a homework hotline to provide support to students and parents who were encountering difficulties, introduction of a Saturday

Learning Club to provide additional time for learning, and implementation of flexible learning groups in targeting needed skills. Our goal was to help the faculty develop a better understanding of and commitment to the school improvement plan.

For this carouseling activity, we divided the faculty into five teams of six members each. We gave them 10 minutes to set up their charts, following these directions:

- Write your school improvement plan component on your chart.
- Below the component, provide a simple definition for it.
- Write a statement that outlines how this component will help improve the achievement of the students.

Each of the groups of travelers visited all four of the other charts, and the travelers provided suggestions to clarify and improve the explanations of how each plan component would increase student achievement. Since the stayers did not have a chance to view the other charts, we gave all members a chance to walk around and look at the work done during the carouseling process before we completed the small group discussions.

SOURCE: From *Energizing Staff Meetings* (pp. 67–69), by S. Eller and J. Eller, 2006, Thousand Oaks, CA: Corwin. Copyright 2006 by Corwin. Adapted with permission.

STRATEGY: LEAFING OUT WITH GOAL ATTAINMENT

To prepare for this strategy, make a large tree out of paper and attach it to a wall in your staff lounge. On colored leaves, write all of the positive things that are occurring at your building. You also could celebrate the goals that you have reached as a building by putting each goal on a leaf and placing it on the tree. Leaves for the goals that your building is working on can be placed at the bottom of the tree to show you are working on the goals. It is important that your goals be specific and clear enough so that staff can tell when you have attained them.

This strategy helps people to see the progress they have made so far and to look at what is left for them to accomplish. It provides a good visual to help people to "see" what has been completed. We have found that staff members have looked forward to seeing another leaf placed on the tree. At times, we have placed the leaves during staff meetings and used the event as a reason for celebration. We have even asked staff members who have been key to the accomplishment of a goal to place that goal's leaf on the tree.

For some staff members, a tree may not hold a lot of meaning. For these people, you might consider something else that can be built upon that has meaning for them, such as a plant with flowers, a tower, a house foundation, a pathway, or something else visual.

Figure 6.2   Sample Movement Pattern for Carouseling

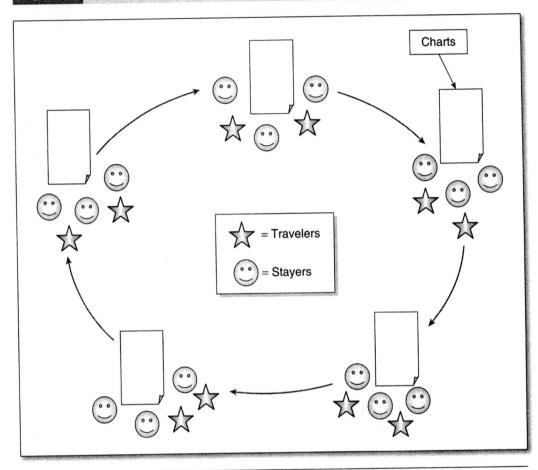

SOURCE: Eller & Eller (2006, p. 93).

Even though this type of strategy sounds simple, it brings meaning and positive emotions to the goal accomplishment process. It can pay big dividends with a staff. It can help them to overcome the perception that goal attainment is boring and just a lot of work and allow them to have fun and celebrate their accomplishments. It can be used at the classroom level to help motivate students as well as at the adult level to motivate staff members.

SOURCE: From *Energizing Staff Meetings* (p. 110), by S. Eller and J. Eller, 2006, Thousand Oaks, CA: Corwin. Copyright 2006 by Corwin. Adapted with permission.

ACTIVITY: COMPARISON DIAGRAM

The use of a comparison diagram is a visual facilitation technique that helps to energize a group and assist their processing. Here it is used in helping a group examine the similarities and differences among ideas, concepts, or decisions, but it can be used for a variety of other purposes with a group. This exercise is helpful because it allows the team members to generate ideas in an objective fashion, and it helps them to develop a visual representation of the information they may be examining more closely in the future.

Activity Directions:

- Post a grid or diagram such as those in the examples that follow, using the topics to be discussed as column headings.

- The group can work as a whole or break into small teams to talk about the components on the grid.

- The group sums up its learning by filling in the blocks of the grid, as shown in the examples below.

Topic	Block Scheduling	6-Period Day	7-Period Day
Similarities			
Differences			

- In this example, the team would list the ways in which each major scheduling type is similar to or different from the school's current approach to scheduling.

Topic	Block Scheduling	6-Period Day	7-Period Day
Match with existing school practices			
New learning or structures that would be required to make the idea successful			

- In this second example, a different way to use a comparison diagram is illustrated: The major topics remain the same as in the first example, but the processing that is required of the participants is different. Here, they are being asked to look at the topics from a perspective of ease of implementation. After a team has completed this diagram, they would clearly understand the issues that might be associated with implementing a new idea.

Materials/Supplies Needed:

- Posted grids with appropriate headings
- Pens, pencils, markers

While these ideas may look very simple, they can be powerful in helping a group to objectively examine several issues and to truly understand the scope of the issues. Some facilitators will hold an open dialog where people work together as one group on the diagram; others may divide the larger team into small groups, each working on one topic within the diagram; other groups may be asked to complete the entire diagram without facilitator guidance. However it is completed, it is important to have the group talk about the completed diagram and make any changes that the entire group feels need to be made so that it reflects current thought. It is also a good idea for a group to talk about what they have learned as a result of the activity once it is completed.

SOURCE: Adapted from Eller & Eller (2006).

ACTIVITY: BUY WHAT IS MOST IMPORTANT

This strategy, although simple in nature, provides an energizing way to help staff member groups to set priorities for tasks and ideas.

Activity Directions:

• At the beginning of the meeting, provide each staff member with a set amount of play money. Think about what you want them to prioritize, then issue an amount of play money that will help them narrow their choices.

• Let the staff members know that after a discussion of all possible ideas or strategies to be explored at the meeting, they will have a chance to bid on their top two choices from the list generated through the discussion.

• Write all of the possible solutions on a chart tablet, and ask staff members to think about their top choices for implementation from the list.

• Ask staff members to place the amount of play money they would "pay" for each choice in envelopes that have been attached to the chart near the choices.

• Count the amount of money in each envelope. The top money getters are the prioritized choices; those with the lowest amounts of money are eliminated from the list.

Materials/Supplies Needed:

• Chart paper and stand
• Pens, pencils, markers
• Envelopes and a means of attaching them to the chart
• Play money

There are many ways to vary this activity. You are limited only by your creativity and your ability to try new things with your staff members to keep this activity energizing and fun. Here are some of the most common variations of this idea that we have seen or implemented:

Auction. Identify a staff member as an auctioneer, and conduct an open auction to see which ideas get the most money or interest.

Credit card bidding. Instead of issuing money to teachers, provide each staff member with an amount of credit to be used in the bidding process. Allow staff members to trade and exchange their credits to prioritize the tasks.

Hidden costs. Have staff members talk about the "hidden costs" of the different tasks listed; some of the choices may cost more money to implement than others. When staff members are asked to place bids on the items, they must take into account the hidden costs of the tasks. Those items with more hidden costs will need a larger bid to be selected. For example, a choice with more hidden costs may take a minimum bid of $5 from each interested party, whereas an idea with minimal hidden costs may take a minimum of bid of only $1 from each interested party. You can determine the hidden cost of a choice or have the group members assist in determining the hidden cost through conversations and consensus.

Group bidding. Allow staff members to get together in teams and combine their money as a group to "purchase" their top choices. However, it is important to be careful with this strategy to avoid allowing groups to bid against each other if this will cause hard feelings.

SOURCE: From *Energizing Staff Meetings* (pp. 69–70), by S. Eller and J. Eller, 2006, Thousand Oaks, CA: Corwin. Copyright 2006 by Corwin. Adapted with permission.

ACTIVITY: IT'S A STAR

When any group of staff members is asked to generate a list of possible solutions to a problem or to develop the next steps in a planning process, some of the ideas carry more importance than others. The "It's a Star" activity allows teachers to see that certain items need to have a higher level of consideration than others.

Activity Directions:

- Have team members generate a list of possible ideas or solutions to a problem; designate one team member to write the solutions on posted chart paper or on cards placed on a table.

- Once all of the possible ideas are listed, ask team members to clarify any ideas or items on the list that the group does not understand.

- Once everyone understands all of the ideas, give each team member a set of large gold stars; one star should have a "5" written on it, another a "4," and a third a "3." The set should also include three stars that have no numbers written on them.

- Ask team members to put the 5 star on the idea that is their top choice, the 4 star by their second choice, and the 3 star by their third choice. They can place their unnumbered stars by any of the possible choices.

- Once everyone has had a chance to place their stars, report the results; the group now holds a discussion about their thoughts in relation to the activity.

- Once the discussion is finished, ask team members if any of them would like to move their stars. Any who are interested in moving their stars are given the opportunity to do so.

- The group engages in another discussion about the process and the results of their star placement and then makes a decision about the prioritization of the items on their list. Obviously, the ideas with the most stars or the stars that total the most points are selected as the top priorities for implementation.

Materials/Supplies Needed:

- Chart paper or cards
- Markers
- Numbered and unnumbered stars or star stickers

SOURCE: From *Energizing Staff Meetings* (pp. 70–71), by S. Eller and J. Eller, 2006, Thousand Oaks, CA: Corwin. Copyright 2006 by Corwin. Adapted with permission.

ACTIVITY: CRITERIA RATING

In this variation of "It's a Star," team members are asked to rate the ideas generated during a group process, but they are required to use agreed-upon criteria. In order to develop a clear and objective rating system, team members need to think about what is needed to solve the problem when looking at possible solutions. In our work with groups over the years, we have found that teachers can benefit from evaluating possible choices against clear criteria. Once you help them to develop this kind of thinking, you will find that their solutions become well thought out and focused.

Activity Directions:

- Identify an issue or problem, and have your team members develop a list of possible ideas or solutions by brainstorming.

- Allow them time to ask for clarification of any items from the list that are unclear.

- Tell the teachers they will have a chance to prioritize their ideas, but first, you want them to develop the criteria they will use in this prioritization process.

- Ask teachers to work in small groups to generate a list of criteria they will use to prioritize their choices. Provide them with some starter ideas, such as the impact on the school's mission, the cost of implementation, short-term versus long-term ideas, ease of implementation, and so forth.

- Have each small group write its prioritization criteria on another chart tablet or white board. Once all of the groups have written their ideas down, hold a discussion about which criteria the group thinks will best help them to prioritize their list.

- Using the same process as described in the "It's a Star" activity, ask the team members to use the stars they have been given to rate the possible ideas or solutions.

- Once all of the ideas have been rated, engage the teachers in a discussion about the process and the results. Be sure they use the criteria they developed to rate the choices in their discussions.

- Develop a plan to move forward on the top choices of the group members.

Materials/Supplies Needed:

- Chart paper or whiteboard
- Markers
- Numbered and unnumbered stars or star stickers

SOURCE: From *Energizing Staff Meetings* (pp. 71–72), by S. Eller and J. Eller, 2006, Thousand Oaks, CA: Corwin. Copyright 2006 by Corwin. Adapted with permission.

ACTIVITY: PROGRESSIVE PROBLEM SOLVING

This activity is unique because team members build on each other's ideas and solutions.

Activity Directions:

- Divide a large group into smaller teams of three to four people.

- Designate a Team One, Team Two, and so forth, until all the teams have numbers.

- Share the problem in a written form with Team One. This team has 2 minutes to read the problem and to write a possible solution to the problem.

- Once the 2 minutes have elapsed, Team One needs to pass its problem and solution to Team Two; this team has 3 minutes to read and understand the problem plus the solution generated by Team One. It must write two possible solutions to add to the list of ideas.

- Once the 3 minutes have elapsed, Team Two must pass the sheet to Team Three; this group must read and understand the problem and the solutions generated by the other teams. Team Three has 4 minutes to add three possible solutions to the list of ideas generated by the other teams.

- The process is repeated until all of the teams have had a chance to add ideas to the original list.

- The original list is given back to Team One, all of the ideas on the list are discussed in the large group, and the most desirable solutions are selected by the large group.

Materials/Supplies Needed:

- Sheet with problem written on it and plenty of room to write solutions
- Pens or pencils

Although the directions for this activity show only one problem being taken through the process, multiple problems can be addressed simultaneously. Each team can be given a different problem to start with, and the problems can be passed around until all teams have had a chance to address all of the problems.

SOURCE: From *Energizing Staff Meetings* (pp. 74–75), by S. Eller and J. Eller, 2006, Thousand Oaks, CA: Corwin. Copyright 2006 by Corwin. Adapted with permission.

ACTIVITY: FROM MY PERSPECTIVE

An important aspect of problem solving is looking at a problem from multiple perspectives. When teams can do this, they are able to anticipate some of the situations that normally cause other problems during the initial stages of implementation of a solution to the initial problem. This activity uses a graphic that helps team members to examine the problem and its solutions from a variety of perspectives. In implementing this activity, use a chart similar to the one illustrated in Figure 6.3.

Activity Directions:

• Post a clear description of the problem faced by the group or the organization in the center of the chart.

• Around the outside of the chart, list the different perspectives that need to be considered in generating solutions and ideas. For example, perspectives might include those of students, teachers, parents, administrative staff, and community members.

• One at a time, list the unique needs of each perspective, and then list the possible solutions that might be generated by a group with this perspective.

• After all of the perspectives have been addressed, talk about the possible solutions that the staff members need to adopt to address the concern or problem.

Materials/Supplies Needed:

• Chart paper with description of the problem
• Markers

SOURCE: From *Energizing Staff Meetings* (pp. 75–76), by S. Eller and J. Eller, 2006, Thousand Oaks, CA: Corwin. Copyright 2006 by Corwin. Adapted with permission.

ACTIVITY: RIPPLE EFFECTS

Normally, school-based teams don't always consider the external impact of their decisions. This activity can help energize the group and allows members a chance to consider all of the ripple effects of their decisions. The use of a visual tool also helps to energize a group of people and to allow them to "see" the impacts of their possible decisions. A sample of a chart that we have used with groups is depicted in Figure 6.4.

You don't have to be a great artist to draw a chart such as this. We usually draw our charts so that the ripples are not evenly spaced from the center or cause. This is purposeful, because we want the team members to know that the ripple effects for certain groups or individuals may come at different times or distances from the event or action.

Activity Directions:

• Have the group members generate a list of possible ideas or problem solutions.

Figure 6.3   From My Perspective

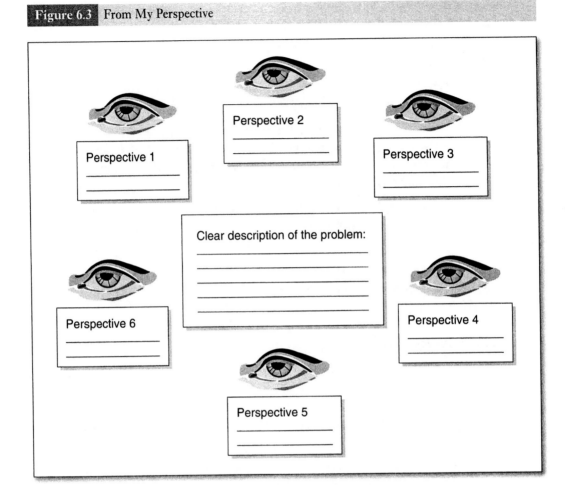

SOURCE: Eller & Eller (2006).

- Work with the group to narrow the list down to two or three ideas that may have some merit in solving the problem.

- Using one ripple chart for each suggestion or idea, write the idea or suggestion in the center space.

- Engage the group members in brainstorming all of the possible effects of the suggestion or idea. Write these effects in the box in the lower left corner of the chart.

- Once all of the potential effects have been listed, have the group members discuss where they should be placed on the chart; the distance from the center represents how quickly the ripple effect would be felt or the relative strength of the effect on the affected party.

- After the whole group has had a chance to analyze the ripple effects, identify a group leader to guide a discussion about what the group learned in the process and what they want to do.

Materials/Supplies Needed:

- Chart paper
- Markers

A group of teachers we recently led through this process developed the ripple effects depicted in Figure 6.5. Only a sample of the ripple effects identified are included in the example.

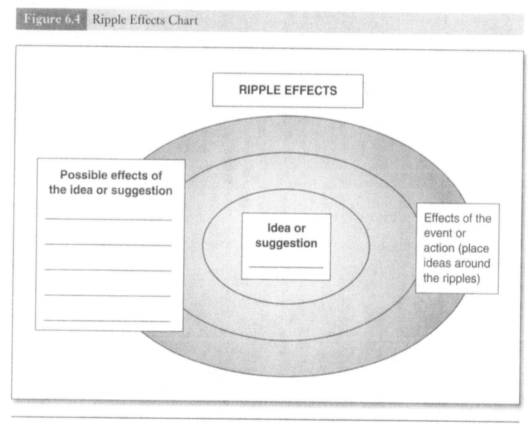

Figure 6.4 Ripple Effects Chart

SOURCE: Eller & Eller (2006, p. 87).

ACTIVITY: SMALL GROUP RIPPLE EFFECTS

A simple variation of the large-group Ripple Effects activity involves breaking the large group into smaller teams to talk about the relative impact of the ideas or suggestions.

Activity Directions:

- Divide a larger group into smaller teams consisting of two or three people each.

Figure 6.5 Example of a Completed Ripple Effects Chart

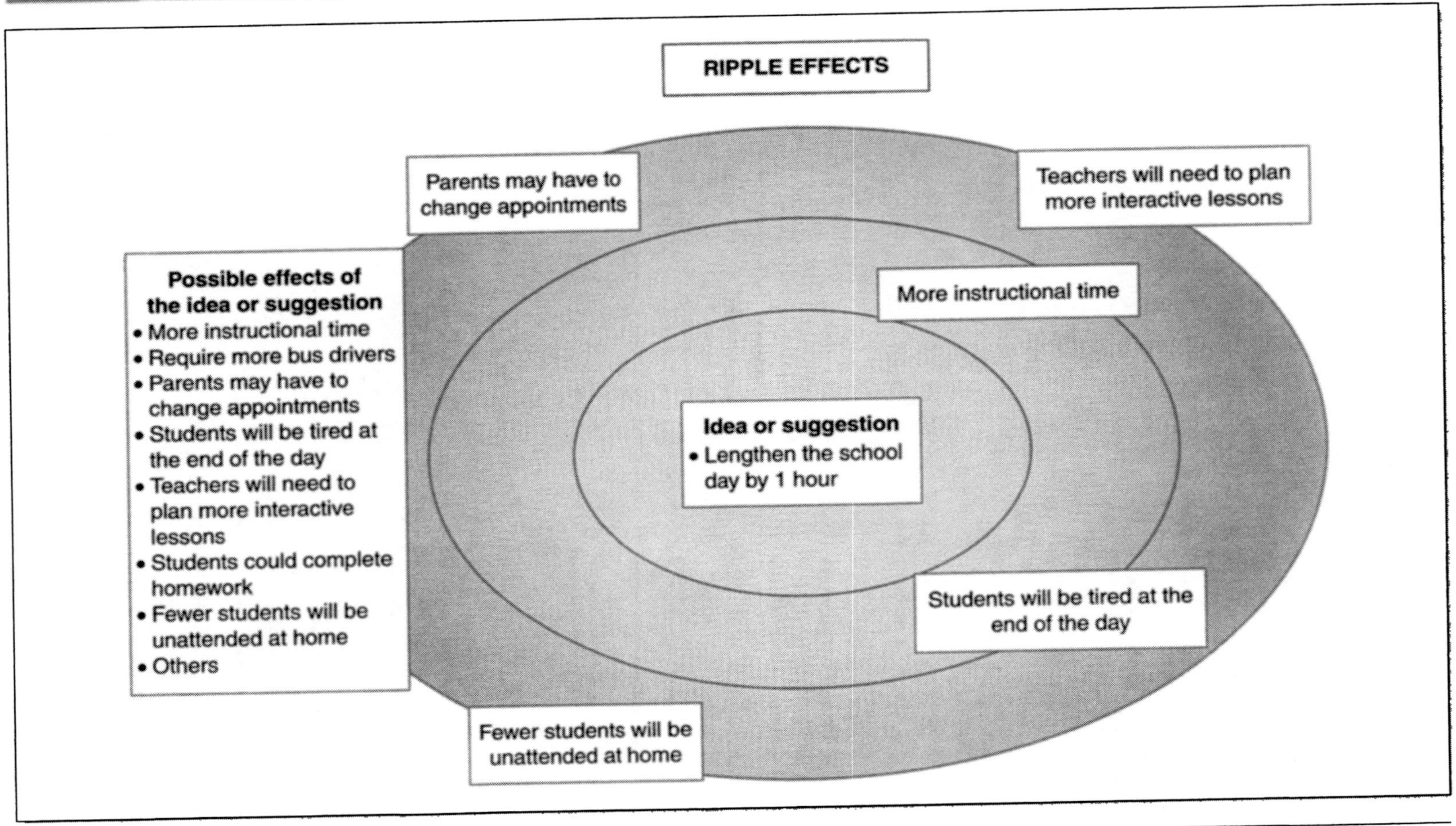

RIPPLE EFFECTS

Teachers will need to plan more interactive lessons

More instructional time

Students will be tired at the end of the day

Parents may have to change appointments

Idea or suggestion
• Lengthen the school day by 1 hour

Fewer students will be unattended at home

Possible effects of the idea or suggestion
• More instructional time
• Require more bus drivers
• Parents may have to change appointments
• Students will be tired at the end of the day
• Teachers will need to plan more interactive lessons
• Students could complete homework
• Fewer students will be unattended at home
• Others

SOURCE: Eller & Eller (2006, p. 89).

- Give each of these smaller teams a copy of the ripple effects chart, and ask them to generate a set of effects and to place them on the "ripples" in relation to their impact. Have all of the small teams work from the *same idea* or suggestion.

- Once all of the groups have finished, have small teams pair with other small teams to have a dialogue about their ideas and placements.

- Bring the entire group back together in a large group to talk about the ideas generated and the processing that occurred in the smaller groups.

- Have the large group use the information that was generated during the activity to make decisions regarding the implementation of the ideas or suggestions generated.

Materials/Supplies Needed:

- Copies of Ripple Effects chart
- Markers

A variation on this activity works in much the same manner, except that each of the small groups is assigned a *different idea* or suggestion to analyze. Once all of the groups have completed their small ripple effects charts, they come together to talk about their analyses of the ideas and suggestions. The entire group is involved in making a decision about the implementation of the ideas or suggestions generated and analyzed during this process.

ACTIVITY: STICKY NOTE RIPPLE EFFECTS

Another variation that has become quite popular with groups involves using sticky notes to gather and post possible ripple effects for new implementations. This variation allows group members to work independently but combine their ideas together to truly identify the impacts of a program or decision.

Activity Directions:

- Give each group member four to five sticky notes.

- Once the idea or suggestion is listed on the large chart, give individuals 2 to 3 minutes to list as many ripple effects as possible, writing each one on a sticky note.

- Once the time has expired, ask group members to come up to the chart and place their ripple effects to show their relative impact. All of the individuals can come up at once to place their sticky notes on the chart, or they can take turns.

Materials/Supplies Needed:

- Chart paper
- Markers
- Sticky notes
- Pens or pencils

This is a quick and energizing way to help people to process the impact of their ideas and suggestions.

ACTIVITY: RIPPLE EFFECTS CONTEST

Often, teachers like to have some type of competition associated with their work. Introducing competition can be fun, but you need to consider the benefits of competition versus the costs to the collaborative needs of the group members. Assuming that a little competition will be fun for the group, you may consider offering this variation.

Activity Directions:

- Divide the larger group into smaller teams of three or four people.

- Give each group a set of colored sticky notes; each small group's sticky notes should be all the same color, and that color should be different from the color of all of the other small groups' sticky notes.

- Post the ripple effects chart on the wall so that all of the group members can see it, and explain the idea or suggestion listed on the chart.

- Allow the small groups 5 minutes to generate as many ripple effects as they can think of and to write each one on a sticky note.

- At the end of the 5-minute time limit, ask a representative from each small group to post his or her group's sticky notes on the large ripple effects chart at the front of the room.

- Each team earns a point for each unique idea that is generated on the chart. A unique idea means that the idea was not identified by any other group during the process. Post the scores for each team; the winning team earns some small prize for its efforts.

- After the point total has been determined, the entire group talks about the ideas generated and their placement on the ripple effects chart.

- Using what they learned in the activity, the group makes a decision regarding the implementation of the idea or suggestion.

Materials/Supplies Needed:

- Chart paper
- Markers
- Sticky notes in a variety of colors
- Pens or pencils

ACTIVITY: CAROUSEL RIPPLE EFFECTS

This variation of the basic concept can be fun and energizing for participants.

Activity Directions:

- Divide the larger group into smaller teams of four or five people.

- Assign each of the smaller teams one idea or suggestion that they will analyze for ripple effects. Give each of these small teams a chart similar to the one shown in Figure 6.4.

- Set a time limit of 10 minutes for the first part of the activity. During this time period, the small teams need to talk about their idea or suggestion, make sure they understand it, and generate as many ripple effects as they can think of relating to their assigned idea or suggestion. Their ripple effects need to be written on the chart and placed in the ripple that shows the effects' relative impact.

- At the end of the 10-minute development period, ask each team to designate two traveling members. The rest of the team members will stay at the chart they helped to develop.

- At your signal, have the travelers move to the next team and its chart. Before giving the signal, designate a movement pattern (have all of the travelers move in the same direction; it could be clockwise or counter-clockwise) and the amount of time for each cycle of the traveling process. (See Figure 6.2 for an illustration of the movement pattern.)

- When the travelers reach a new team, their job is to listen to a brief (1-minute) explanation of that team's work by the team members still at the chart. Once the explanation has been heard, the travelers are required to add two more ripple effects to the chart they are visiting. These new ripple effects need to be written on the chart by the travelers.

- After three or four visitations, stop the activity and ask the travelers to return to their home teams. Have the home teams talk about what the travelers and the stayers learned as a result of the activity.

- The small teams are asked to share the results of their dialogue with the large group.

- The large group makes a decision about the implementation of the ideas or suggestions as a result of the activity.

Materials/Supplies Needed:

- Copies of Ripple Effects chart
- Markers

SOURCE: From *Energizing Staff Meetings* (pp. 86–92), by S. Eller and J. Eller, 2006, Thousand Oaks, CA: Corwin. Copyright 2006 by Corwin. Adapted with permission.

SUMMARY

In this chapter, you have seen a wide variety of activities and strategies that allow you to improve the culture of your faculty group by increasing collaboration while getting important tasks and work completed. Since there are a wide variety of activities presented, you should have been able to find at least one or two activities that you would be comfortable in implementing at your school. As you reflect on the content of this chapter, please review the following:

- What did you see in common across the activities presented?
- How might you be able to modify activities in order to help them better meet the needs of your group?
- How do you think your faculty group would benefit from using these strategies to resolve issues in a collaborative manner?

In the next chapter, Building a Sense of Team, we will examine ideas and strategies that you will find useful in improving the culture of your school through team-building. Team-building can be an important aspect of a comprehensive school culture improvement project, and we know you will find rich and interesting activities in this chapter to assist you in this effort.

7

Building a Sense of Team

S o far, we have talked a lot about activities that can be integrated into the normal operations of a school to improve climate and culture. Another set of activities and ideas that can be implemented to improve climate and culture are physical and mental team-building activities.

ABOUT THIS CHAPTER

Team-building activities are important to an overall program that is designed to improve the climate and culture of a school. We have used team-building activities in all of our schools to help teachers learn how to work together and create a positive culture. As you review the activities presented in this chapter, reflect on the following questions:

- What is the importance of building community in efforts to improve climate and culture?
- What physical and mental team-building activities seem to work in improving climate and culture?
- How can teachers learn from team-building through processing and application?
- What activities and strategies would be best suited to my staff and their unique needs?

INTERDEPENDENCE, COMMUNITY, AND THEIR IMPACT ON SCHOOL CLIMATE AND CULTURE

In the book, *Effective Group Facilitation in Education: How to Energize Meetings and Manage Difficult Groups,* John Eller outlines the following related to improving the climate and culture of a school:

> When a group is operating in an interdependent manner, it is working together for good of the group while maintaining the identities of the individuals on the team. This blend of individual and team creates a condition that many change agents call "synergy." (Eller, 2004, p. 74)

ACTIVITY: TOXIC WASTE TRANSFER

The toxic waste transfer task requires the group to transport objects across an open space without directly touching the objects or their container. The group will manipulate a bucket filled with small objects using ropes attached to the bucket.

Activity Directions:

- The group members form a circle around a five-gallon bucket. This bucket has numerous ropes attached to it (see picture in materials/supplies list). The group members must hold onto the ends of the ropes.

- Place the bucket approximately 50 to 60 feet from another container that is large enough to hold the entire contents of the original bucket.

- Working together, the group transports the bucket from one spot to another by manipulating the ropes. The group also uses these ropes to transfer the contents of the bucket to another container.

- Discuss the following rules with your group:
  o The group may use only the ropes to move and transfer the waste; if a group member touches the bucket or the waste, the group must go back to the beginning and start over.
  o Once the bucket is picked up by the group, it cannot be set down until the waste is transferred.
  o If any waste spills in the movement or transfer process, the group must select a waste clean up specialist who will put all the waste back into the original bucket. Then the group must start the process over again from the beginning.
  o Each rope on the bucket must have at least one person holding it, and each person on the team must be touching at least one rope.

○ Team members may not be any closer to the bucket than half the length of the rope.

Materials/Supplies Needed:

- A toxic waste transfer bucket. Take an empty five-gallon bucket, and drill between 15 and 20 small holes randomly in the sides. Thread ropes of at least eight feet in length through the holes, and tie a knot on the inside end of each rope. Your bucket should look like the example pictured below.
- For the toxic waste, fill the bucket with tennis balls, golf balls, Styrofoam peanuts, or other material that can be poured in an efficient manner.

The task is concluded when all of the material has been transferred from the original container to the second container. Debrief the activity by asking team members to talk about what they learned about each other and the team as a result of this activity.

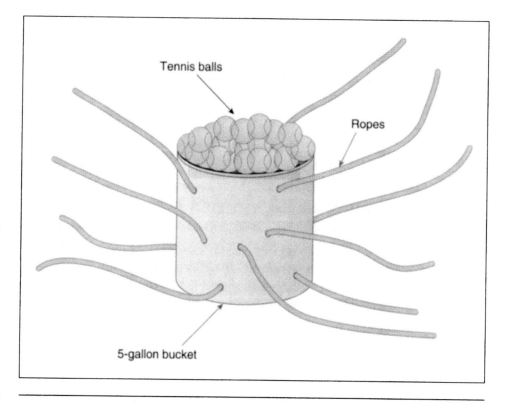

SOURCE: From *Effective Group Facilitation in Education: How to Energize Meetings and Manage Difficult Groups* (pp. 77–78), by J. Eller, 2004, Thousand Oaks, CA: Corwin. Copyright 2004 by Corwin. Adapted with permission.

ACTIVITY: FIGURE IT OUT

Figure It Out is an activity that helps educators to get to know each other on a deeper level while playing on teachers' natural talents for doing what they do best—getting up in front of groups. The activity also gets people to think and problem-solve, plus it provides for movement.

Activity Directions:

- Divide the staff into small teams of three to five people.
- Give each of the teams a card that contains a words, phrase, or idea they are to illustrate using some type of skit or action.
  - o You can use educational concepts such as accountability, collective bargaining, the first day of school, giving a test, and so forth.
  - o You can use generic ideas such as summer vacation, getting married, building a house, warm sunlight, and so forth.
- Give each of the teams 5 minutes to plan out their action or skit. Each skit needs to be nonverbal in nature, using no spoken or written clues.
- As each team presents its skit or action, the remainder of the group tries to guess the word or phrase represented by the action or skit.
- Record how long it takes the larger group to guess the word or phrase represented by each skit. Give a prize to the group whose word or phrase is guessed correctly in the shortest amount of time.

Materials/Supplies Needed:

- Cards with phrases, words, or ideas

ACTIVITY: COMMUNICATION PROBLEMS

Communication Problems is an important activity for helping to build a team. This activity builds communication skills among group members. It emphasizes the importance of speaking and listening. This challenge can be done with limited space and materials.

Activity Directions:

- Have team members sit in either a semicircle or randomly in an area.
- Have the group select one member as the communication manager. This person stands in front of the group and attempts to describe a picture in terms that will allow group members to draw the objects being described.

- This communication manager may not use certain terms describing standard shapes, such as *circle, square, rectangle,* or *triangle.*

- The group may not ask the communication manager any questions or request further descriptions.

Materials/Supplies Needed:

- A pencil and one piece of paper for each group member for each drawing
- Relatively simple pictures for communication managers to describe
- A clipboard to be used under the picture so that group members cannot see through the paper and copy the drawing

Once the picture has been fully described, the activity is over. Group members share the products of their drawings with each other. The sharing of the drawing can promote some fun and interesting discussions between team members. This on its own can be something that will promote community in itself. Participants in this activity tend to laugh, comment on each other's drawings, and have fun in general.

SOURCE: Adapted from Eller (2004).

ACTIVITY: ALL TIED UP

This physical challenge helps to make participants aware of the difficulty associated with nonverbal communication and helps them to be more aware of problem-solving skills other than the verbal skills normally used by teams. It provides a group the opportunity to work on its collaborative problem-solving skills and learn how to develop alternatives to its verbal or linguistic communication skills.

Activity Directions:

- Place group members in a single file line, and ask them to hold onto a rope that is about 100 feet long. The rope should have between 10 and 12 knots tied in it at equidistant intervals. Each group member must hold onto the rope with one hand.

- The object of the activity is to have the group untie all the knots in the rope while the members are still holding onto it.

- Group members may all face the same direction, or they can face in different directions; the important thing to remember is that group members must not let go of the rope in accomplishing the task.

- The group will need to do the activity in a room that has enough space to spread out a little in order to have the room it needs in order to move around in untying the knots.

Materials/Supplies Needed:

- A soft rope about a half-inch in diameter and 100 feet long. You will need to tie 10 to 12 loose knots equally spaced along the length of the rope.
- This length of rope is perfect for a group of about a dozen people. Divide larger groups into smaller teams, and provide each with a separate space and rope to do the activity.

Since members cannot let go of the rope to untie it, they will need to enlarge the knots and pass their bodies through them. Once all the knots are out of the rope, the activity is finished. After the rope is free, engage the team in a dialog about the activity and what they learned as a result of the process. Be sure to have them talk about how the dynamics were shaped by the fact that they were unable to verbally communicate during the activity.

SOURCE: From *Effective Group Facilitation in Education: How to Energize Meetings and Manage Difficult Groups* (pp. 79–80), by J. Eller, 2004, Thousand Oaks, CA: Corwin. Copyright 2004 by Corwin. Adapted with permission.

ACTIVITY: PASSING THE HOOP

This activity provides a group with a lot of fun and lets people relax a little and get to know each other in a deeper and more meaningful manner.

Activity Directions:

- Divide a large group into smaller groups of 8 to 10 people, and ask them to stand in a circle facing each other.
- Tell group members to join hands, and then hang a hula hoop on one of the pairs of hands that are joined.
- Group members should make the hula hoop travel around the circle. (In order to do this, the hoop must go over people's heads, and group members must step through the bottom of the hoop.)
- Group members can cheer each other along or provide details about how to accomplish the task, but they may not release their grips on each other's hands.

Materials/Supplies Needed:

- A hula hoop for each small group

At the end of the activity, group members are asked to talk about what they learned as a result of the activity and how it will benefit them as they work together as a group.

ACTIVITY: BUILDING A POKER HAND

This simple, but effective team-building activity gets people to mingle, connect with others, and learn more about each other. It can be implemented with medium to large groups.

Activity Directions:

- Give each group member 5 playing cards from a standard 52-card deck.

- Ask team members to gain information from other team members by asking them questions. Some sample information you may have team members obtain could include the following:
   o What made them interested in getting into education
   o A funny story about a recent interaction they have had with children
   o An interesting hobby
   o Their educational background
   o Their favorite relaxation activity

- Provide a signal or timer to alert team members to start interacting with another person in the room. Provide a short time for the interaction, and then give the signal to move on to another interaction.

- Each time two team members interact, they must trade playing cards. The best situation for a trade is when each staff member agrees to trade a card the other staff member desires. If two staff members cannot quickly agree on a trade, they must each shuffle their cards, place them face down, and allow each other to select a card at random from their card set.

- Team members should try to get cards that will build a winning poker hand. The person with the highest hand at the end of a short time period is declared the winner. It may take several rounds for an individual to collect a good hand.

- At the end of a reasonable amount of time, stop the activity, clarify the winning order of poker hands (i.e., royal flush, straight flush, four of a kind, full house, straight, three of a kind, two pair, one pair), and ask members to share their hands with the group. Involve the group in determining the winning hand or hands.

Materials/Supplies Needed:

- A standard deck of playing cards.
- A set of questions for team members to ask each other, printed on sheets of paper or on a board where all can see them.
- If the group is large, you may need to use two decks to make sure everyone gets five cards; if the group is on the small side, you may need to give members more than five cards.

As you plan this activity, select questions that will let team members learn interesting and helpful things about their peers and that will also contribute to the working relationships of the group. Be sure to think about ideas that will be meaningful and accepted by the group. Be careful in the initial stages about getting too personal too fast.

Provide some type of simple prize at the end for the winner. Thank the group for their participation. Have the group debrief the activity, highlighting what they have learned about their peers and the team as a result of this activity. Ask them to share how they can use this information as they continue to work together in the future. Periodically refer to what they have learned in this activity as they work together in the future.

SOURCE: Adapted from Newstrom & Scannell (1998).

ACTIVITY: HULA HOOP RELAYS

This activity allows group members a chance to show off their talents while supporting each other though a somewhat difficult task. The relay is designed to be difficult and challenging but fun. The activity works best in a gym or large cafeteria.

Activity Directions:

- Before starting the activity, set up the course. The diagram in Figure 7.1 illustrates the course setup.

- Divide a larger group into smaller teams with even numbers of team members—four to six people.

- Have half of the members of each team line up at one end of a room; this line serves as the start/finish line. The others go to another line about 50 feet away.

- Using small sticks (we use paint stir sticks that we obtain from hardware stores), team members take turns rolling a hula hoop from their start line to their team members across the room. The hula hoop must be rolled with the stick, and it must be kept in an upright position.

| Figure 7.1 | Hula Hoop Relay Course Setup |

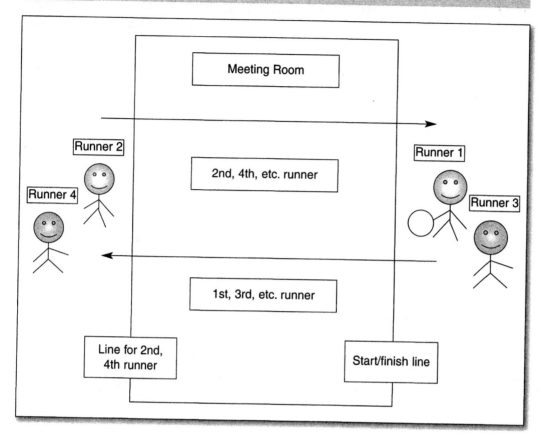

- When a team member reaches the far side of the room, another team member starts to roll the hula hoop back. The receiving team member may not start to roll the hoop until the arriving team member's body goes past the line on which the receiving member is standing. At this point the stick is passed to the receiving team member along with the hula hoop.

- The relay continues until the last team member from one team crosses the finish line; this team is declared the winner.

- After the activity, team members debrief the activity. They talk about what they learned as a result of the activity and how it will help them as they work together in the future.

Materials/Supplies Needed:

- A hula hoop for each team
- A stick for each team

ACTIVITY: CIRCLE OF SUPPORT

Faculty members in a climate where they feel a sense of interdependence tend to engage in more positive communication and relations. The activity Circle of Support reinforces the idea that it takes the entire group to carry the heavy weight of operating the school and making a positive difference in the lives of students. The activity provides a powerful visual representation of this principle for faculty.

Activity Directions:

- Lay out a large, thick piece of rope in a circle on a gym or cafeteria floor. The rope should be long enough to make a circle large enough so that each staff member can hold onto the rope with both hands while facing into the circle. The rope should also be fairly thick and stiff; about one to one-and-one-half inches thick.

- Ask all of the group members to stand around the outside of the rope facing the inside of the circle (see Figure 7.2).

- Ask group members to grab the rope with two hands and pick it up so it is suspended at approximately chest level of the participants.

- Direct group members to stretch the rope tight, trying to form a completely round circle. This can be accomplished by having the group members lean back toward the outside of the circle.

- Now go around the circle and tell some group members to let go of the rope. It is important to remove these members randomly from around the circle.

- As people are removed from the rope, the job becomes more difficult until finally just a few people are left doing all of the work of holding up the rope.

- After the exercise, debrief the group members to see what they learned as a result of the activity.

Materials/Supplies Needed:

- Piece of rope one to one-and-one-half inches in diameter

ACTIVITY: RISING TOWER

Effective problem-solving and communication strategies are essential to effective team operation. This activity provides group members an

Figure 7.2   Circle of Support

opportunity to practice and refine both of these skills. This activity can be performed as a whole team or in small subgroups of the larger team.

Activity Directions:

- The object is to build the highest freestanding tower possible using only toothpicks and marshmallows.

- Give each team 15 minutes to plan and construct the tower. Here are the rules:
  - ○ The tower must be able to stand freely for at least 15 seconds in order to be measured for the contest.
  - ○ Participants may use any construction method of their choosing.
  - ○ The tower's height will be measured from the construction surface to its highest point of the tower above the surface.

- At the conclusion of the 15-minute period, stop the groups from building their towers any further.

- Each group may support its tower if necessary until the facilitator comes around to measure it. However, the tower must stand on its own for

15 seconds before it is measured. If the tower moves when support is removed, it must stop moving before it can be measured.

• Plot the heights of all the towers on a chart so that all of the teams can compare their towers with the others. The group with the highest tower is declared the winner.

Materials/Supplies Needed:

- A box of 500 toothpicks for each team
- A bag of mini marshmallows for each team
- A sturdy building surface for each team

If you only have one team building a tower or if you want to eliminate competition between groups, challenge the group(s) to build a tower of a set height. You have to determine a good height, and announce that you want them to work together to build a tower at or beyond that height. The height that a tower can reach varies greatly, but it is not out of the question to find towers that are 20 to 25 centimeters high.

Be sure to spend some time debriefing the activity. Ask the group to reflect on what they learned about each other and their team as a result of the activity. Groups normally find that they are able to identify their processing and communication strengths as a result of this activity.

SOURCE: From *Effective Group Facilitation in Education: How to Energize Meetings and Manage Difficult Groups* (pp. 82–83), by J. Eller, 2004, Thousand Oaks, CA: Corwin. Copyright 2004 by Corwin. Adapted with permission.

ACTIVITY: IT TAKES A VILLAGE

We've all heard the expression that it takes a village to raise a child. This activity is an adaptation of this saying; it uses the combined efforts of several people to accomplish a task. Even though it is simple, it points out the importance of careful team coordination to complete a task.

Activity Directions:

- Divide a larger group into teams of four.
- Ask each team to stand in a small circle facing each other.
- Combine each team into a single unit by tying their hands together with a light string or a strip of paper.
- Provide the teams with construction paper, markers, glue sticks, tape, scissors, and other decorating items.

- Tell teams they have about 10 minutes to construct a village that represents how the school works together to create an atmosphere where students are successful. The team must stay tied up together as they work together to create the village. If the tie around them breaks, the team must stop construction and get the leader to tie them together again.

- Once the time for construction has elapsed, have each team share its village and talk about how it illustrates the school and its efforts to improve student learning.

- Once all of the villages have been shared, ask the team members to debrief the activity and talk about what they have learned as a result of the activity and seeing the villages.

Materials/Supplies Needed:

- String or strips of paper long enough to tie or fasten around the wrists of each group member
- Construction paper, markers, glue sticks, tape, scissors, and other decorating items

SUMMARY

Team-building activities can be very effective in helping to improve the climate and culture of your school. Not only are team-building activities fun, but they help to take people a little out of their comfort zones. When you use team-building activities with your staff, you not only build your team but can begin to understand the various intelligence preferences of your staff. You also provide an opportunity to assist in the learning of staff members by providing active learning and movement. In general, team-building activities are fun and help improve the climate and culture of a school.

8

We're Not Getting Along; Now What?

In their staff meetings, the Voyager High School staff members had difficulty coming to agreement on anything. Their philosophical beliefs were really diverse, and several of the more senior staff members would just talk louder and drown out others who tried to bring up alternative viewpoints. Obviously, these staff members controlled the conversations at staff meetings.

Ken, the principal of Voyager, wanted to get others more involved in the decisions of the school. He started to think about ways to get others involved in staff meetings. He decided to use written activities as a way to process information and get everyone involved. He started his plan by randomly pairing teachers during meetings to talk with each other, first about minor issues, and then moving to more complex issues as they gained experience with the process. Finally, he divided the staff into task forces to look at a new curricular change at the school. Each task force was charged with the job of looking at subparts of the change. He had each task force present their ideas for the curricular change. Once the ideas were presented, the staff used the Sticky Note Ripple Effects strategy to decide on the level of implementation of the project.

The strategy helped the staff have a balanced and collaborative conversation related to the new project. In the end, the staff decided to slow down the implementation of the curricular change in order to gather more data, but everyone had been able to participate in the conversation and decision, an outcome that indicated growth for the staff at Voyager. The staff had gradually learned to work through the conflict that was keeping them from moving forward. The conflict they were experiencing was natural, but it had been keeping them from airing all points of view, whether or not the various viewpoints were in agreement with those of the more senior members of the staff. By making the content of the conversations more evident, the staff was able to move the conflict to a less personal level.

This example illustrates the importance of helping your staff to learn new behaviors and work through their disagreements. By making their conflict more evident through discussing it in pairs, they were able to move it from a personal level to a more substantive level. This is a key in helping groups to work through conflict and making a productive force for decision making. Working through conflict is the focus of this chapter.

ABOUT THIS CHAPTER

Schools that have healthy climates and cultures have processes in place to work through the conflict that inevitably occurs when people are collaboratively involved in the operation of an organization. School staff members tend to shy away from conflict even though they may be causing it behind the scenes. In this chapter we will talk about ideas and strategies that you can implement to help your staff learn how to effectively deal with conflict.

Even though the bulk of this chapter will be focused on activities, we will also discuss several foundational ideas related to improving the school climate where there is conflict and developing new cultural behaviors.

THE NATURE OF CONFLICT

Conflict is a natural part of processes in which people work together. When people are freed up to participate in the governance of their organizations, conflicts will arise. As a leader of a school, you need to find ways to help your group to view this natural level of conflict as part of their work together and to find ways to use this natural conflict as a source of energy.

In our work with schools over the years, we have found two major kinds or types of conflict: affective and substantive (cognitive). *Affective conflict* relates to conflict that is based on personalities. In affective conflict, parties focus their anger on the personalities of those who disagree with them. Affective conflict can be destructive. In *substantive (cognitive) conflict*, the disagreement or conflict is based on varying philosophies or beliefs about the school community.

The activities described here provide a wide variety of approaches to addressing both types of conflict.

ACTIVITY: PACK UP YOUR BAGGAGE

If you are working with a staff that has difficulty getting along with each other, this activity can help them deal with their issues. People need to find a way to get their problems behind them. This activity has been successful in helping teachers to get rid of their "baggage."

Activity Directions:

- Begin by telling the staff members that you are aware there are many issues that need to be dealt with before they can work together.

- Have people write down the issues that are bothering them. You can have the staff share the issues or just have them write them down. It is important that they have a written copy of their concerns, so that they can "place" them later in the activity.

- Let the staff members know that once they have written down the issues, the written pages will be placed in a suitcase, which then will be locked. The team members need to agree that once the issues are locked in the suitcase, they cannot be taken out and used against each other or discussed.

- Encourage the staff members to talk about any issues they feel need to be addressed before the suitcase is closed. This is their chance to resolve the issues before the issues are off limits for discussion.

- Before the suitcase is closed, get a verbal commitment from each staff member that all of the issues in the suitcase need to remain in the suitcase.

- Close the suitcase and lock it to show that it can't be opened again.

Materials/Supplies Needed

- An old used suitcase
- Paper slips
- Pens or pencils

SOURCE: From *Energizing Staff Meetings* (pp. 121–122), by S. Eller and J. Eller, 2006, Thousand Oaks, CA: Corwin. Copyright 2006 by Corwin. Adapted with permission.

ACTIVITY: PARKING LOT MEETING

In schools, informal meetings often take place in parking lots and other locations after formal meetings end—particularly when a formal meeting does not go well. This activity brings such informal meetings inside to make them a part of the formal meeting. It is an activity that can be employed with any group in any context. It can have a positive impact on the school climate and culture, because it asks participants to share what they have perceived has happened during the meeting and how they feel about it. The activity helps to establish group norms and relationships. It can also be used in instances where it appears that a hidden agenda may be operating.

Activity Directions:

- Advise the group that it is important for them to share what's on their minds in order to get all the concerns out on the table.

- Talk about the fact that sometimes informal meetings occur in the parking lot after a scheduled meeting has been completed. Convey that sometimes these informal parking lot meetings allow team members to discuss issues of concern. Share that it is important to discuss concerns inside the meeting.

- Have participants form self-selected groups of three to five members, and direct them to spend the next 8 to 10 minutes discussing whatever is on their minds regarding the topic or topics under discussion in the regular meeting. Each group may select a convenient space for this discussion, such as a corner of the room, a hallway, or even in the parking lot.

- At the end of the 8- to 10-minute period, reconvene the entire group, and have each "parking lot group" share its conversation. Record issues and concerns on chart paper.

- After all the groups have shared the contents of their parking lot meetings, ask the whole group to discuss the implications of the issues and concerns generated by this process. Talk with the group about possible adjustments to the meeting agenda or topics.

Materials/Supplies Needed:

- Chart paper and markers

The Parking Lot Meeting activity helps the group to get their concerns out on the table and deal with them in a productive manner. This helps to improve the climate, because concerns are able to be dealt with in a timely manner. It also helps your school to develop a culture where open dialogue is valued, and behind-the-back conversations are minimized.

From *Leading With the Brain in Mind: 101 Brain-Compatible Practices for Leaders* (pp. 97–98), by M. H. Dickmann, N. Stanford-Blair, and A. Rosati-Bojar, 2004, Thousand Oaks, CA: Corwin. Copyright 2004 by Corwin. Adapted with permission.

ACTIVITY: TRANSFER THE ANGER

Another strategy that helps a group deal with conflict is providing a way for them to express their anger and frustration. Anger can be transferred to inanimate objects. This not only depersonalizes the conflict but provides a way for people to get their emotions off their chests and hopefully move forward. Many of us have used this strategy in working with children but have been reluctant to use it with adults.

Activity Directions:

- Select an object that is strong and durable but can be easily accessed (examples include a punching doll, a punching bag, and a large, strong balloon).

- Talk about the negative energy or situation that is frustrating to the group.

- Share that the negative situation is represented by the object you have selected.

- Allow individuals to bat, hit, or throw the object or attack it however else they wish. As members take out their frustrations on the object, have them verbally share their frustrations with the group.

- After everyone has been given a chance to vent, talk to the group about the value of the activity and how they think the activity has helped them work through their issues.

Materials/Supplies Needed:

- A strong, durable object

ACTIVITY: ASHES TO ASHES

People do benefit from releasing their emotions and anger through visual or ceremonial ways. We have used this activity to help people release a variety of emotions over the years. It has been successful in helping people release anger and has assisted them in letting go of outdated instructional materials and practices as well as other emotional attachments they've had difficulty letting go of. It provides enough of an emotional ceremony to help people move beyond their resistance.

Activity Directions:

• Ask group members to identify the situation or emotional experience that is bothering them.

• Once the situation has been identified, provide members with small slips of paper, and ask them to write notes or messages in relation to the situation. These notes or messages can be personal communications with or about the situation or emotional experience.

• Pass around a metal, stone, or ceramic container. Ask people to place their slips of paper in the container.

• Move to a fire-safe area with the container. Ask the members of the team placing the notes in the container to form a circle around the container at a safe distance from it.

• In this fire-safe area, light the pieces of paper on fire. The people who placed the slips of paper in the container should be able to see the slips of paper burn.

• Once the paper has burned, allow the ashes to cool. Using a metal scoop, take out the ashes. Either scatter them to the wind or bury them somewhere on the school property.

• Ask the group members to share their feelings about the activity in relation to the negative situation or emotion.

Materials/Supplies Needed:

• Fireproof container
• Slips of paper
• Matches
• Metal scoop

ACTIVITY: GO TO YOUR CORNERS

During meetings, issues can come up that cause conflict among the staff members. Staff may not fully explore these issues because of their fear that the ensuing conflict may cause a problem. Even though these staff members are reluctant to talk about their opposing viewpoints, doing so will help them learn how to work with each other to productively deal with and work through conflict. The activity Go to Your Corners can be a good one to help them as they encounter conflicts.

Activity Directions:

• When you perceive a conflict is occurring, try to identify or label the various sides of or perspectives on the conflict.

- Once the perspectives have been identified, designate corners or areas of the room for further discussion of these perspectives.

- Ask staff members to select a corner to go to that represents a perspective that they share in relation to the conflict. If there are staff members who do not identify with one of the perspectives, ask them to either select one of the existing corners, go to a neutral corner, or wait to hear the perspectives presented by the corner groups once they have finished their discussions.

- Once all of the staff members have selected a location, give them a specific amount of time (5 minutes) to talk about the issue from their perspective. Ask them to be ready to outline their points in a written form such as on a chart or marker board.

- Once the allotted time has elapsed, ask each group to present a short (2- to 3-minute) summary of their points. During each presentation, no questions or comments are allowed by any staff members.

- Ask the groups to go back to their respective corners and now talk about the issues from the opposing views presented in the previous part of the exercise. Require each group to talk (and write notes on chart paper or a marker board) about how the perspectives are similar and about the major differences that exist in each perspective. Then ask them to share their understanding of the similarities and differences in a short (2- to 3-minute) presentation at the end of their discussion.

- Each group is allowed to present the product of their latest work to the entire group. After each presentation, open-ended, nonjudgmental questions are allowed. Once each group presents its opinions, they are asked to post their chart for the entire group to examine.

- Depending on the level of agreement that is observed through the presentations and charts, the leader can decide to table the conversation until a later date or continue to talk about how some level of compromise can be reached among the various perspectives.

Materials/Supplies Needed:

- Chart paper (or another writing surface)
- Markers or pens

SOURCE: From *Energizing Staff Meetings* (pp. 76–79), by S. Eller and J. Eller, 2006, Thousand Oaks, CA: Corwin. Copyright 2006 by Corwin. Adapted with permission.

ACTIVITY: CORNER ON PERSPECTIVES

This activity has some similarities to the Go to Your Corner activity just presented, but in this activity, participants are asked to examine the conflict from a different angle. At times, when people are asked to go to a corner and talk about their own perspective, their ownership of the perspective can be reinforced. In this activity, as you send each group to a corner of the room, assign them a unique perspective that they need to consider as they hold their discussion. Here are some of the perspectives that you can ask the small groups to consider:

School district's perspective

Parents' perspective

Students' perspective

Teachers' perspective

Impact on the community

Impact on local businesses

Positive aspects of the problem

Negative aspects of the problem

Economic cost of the solutions

Time costs of the solutions

Worst-case scenarios of the problem and solutions

Best-case scenarios of the problem and solutions

If we do nothing

Holes in the solutions

Whole problem

Details of the problem

Causes of the problem

Ripple effects of the possible solutions

Others, as appropriate

During the various large group interactions, the subgroup members need to present the situation from their unique perspective and work to understand the different unique perspectives held by others in the room. Since this activity is more general in nature than the Go to Your Corners activity outlined earlier, it may be easier to implement for groups just learning how to work with conflict.

SOURCE: Adapted from Eller & Eller (2006).

ACTIVITY: VICTORY LAPS

The victory lap process is a practice that facilitates an emotional orientation to what is going well and is right with the world. It can be conducted in small, medium, or large groups in any context calling for reduction of emotional stress and promotion of positive perspectives. It is an activity that helps to promote a positive school climate and culture, because it focuses teachers on looking at the positive aspects of their lives and school.

Activity Directions:

• Give teachers a topic around which to organize their positive comments.

• Starting in one section of the room and moving progressively from person to person in a regular manner (for example, around a table, around a room, or from front to back rows), have each person say something positive about the topic.

• At the end of the activity, ask the group to meet in pairs to discuss what they learned as a result of the activity.

Materials/Supplies Needed:

• None

SOURCE: From *Leading With the Brain in Mind: 101 Brain-Compatible Practices for Leaders* (pp. 85–86), by M. H. Dickmann, N. Stanford-Blair, and A. Rosati-Bojar, 2004, Thousand Oaks, CA: Corwin. Copyright 2004 by Corwin. Adapted with permission.

ACTIVITY: HALF-FULL OR HALF-EMPTY

Many times, educators look at and focus on the negative aspects of a problem. This negative view can limit their ability to generate creative solutions to the problems they face as a staff. This energizer is designed to help teacher teams to balance the positives and negatives of the problem or challenge they are facing.

Activity Directions:

• At the beginning of the problem-resolution process, put up a chart that shows a drawing of a glass (see Figure 8.1).

- Ask the group to use sticky notes to write down the positive and negative aspects of the problem facing them or the school. Only one idea can be written on each note.

- Ask teachers at random to come up to the chart and place one sticky note on either the positive or negative part of the large glass. The positive aspects or conditions of the problem are placed on the top part of the glass; the negative aspects or conditions of the problem are placed at the bottom of the glass.

- Once all of the sticky notes have been placed on the large glass, review the notes, and ask the teachers to discuss what they learned about the problem and what they want to do as a result of the activity.

Materials/Supplies Needed:

- A large piece of chart paper (with a glass drawn on it)
- Sticky notes to place on the chart/glass
- Pens or pencils

Figure 8.1   Half-Full or Half-Empty

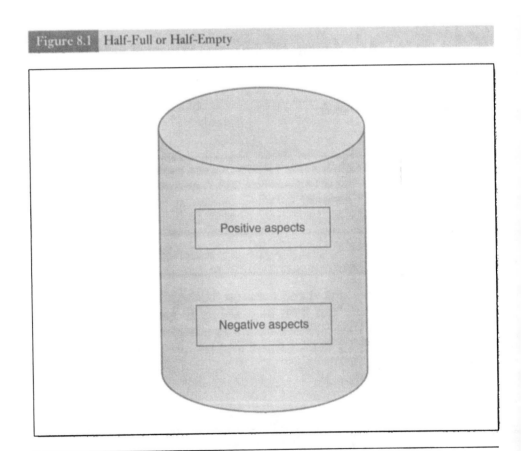

SOURCE: Eller & Eller (2006).

We have used the following variation to the Half-Full or Half-Empty activity with success: We ask teachers to place the positive and negative sticky notes on the chart in an alternating fashion (first a positive note, then a negative note, alternating positive and negative with every other note). This process continues until no more attributes from either the positive or negative side of the issue can be posted; at this point all posting must stop.

This variation requires a team to look at both the positive and negative sides of an issue. From our experience, people have found it easier to generate the negative aspects of a topic or idea. When we require them to keep a balance between the positive and the negative, they are forced to generate positive attributes. This not only keeps the issue balanced in terms of positives and negatives but helps the team develop the habit of looking at both sides of issues in a balanced way. It pays dividends in the long term for teams.

Another approach is to have the team place all of the negative aspects on the chart first, and then move to the positive aspects. For every positive aspect or idea placed on the chart, a negative can be removed. The activity is completed when all of the positive aspects have replaced the negative aspects. This variation also causes people to move beyond the negative aspects of a situation and begin to look at both the positives and the negatives of an issue or idea.

You can also duplicate small versions of the large glass chart and ask individuals or small groups to complete these smaller versions. Then have the small groups combine into larger teams to talk about their products and place sticky notes representing the results of their discussions on the larger glass chart. Hold a large group discussion about the process and the results of working through the exercise.

This variation can be helpful, because it can work to defuse the negative emotions that can be built up in a large group. Since small teams are completing the activity first, then working in slightly larger teams to combine and clarify their thoughts, many of the issues that could come up in a large group setting can be dealt with before they get to the large group. It also allows more interaction and participation by all team members. Many times, we have found that when a negative idea comes up at the small group level, a team member tends to present the positive side of the issue. This can be much more effective than letting negative ideas come up in a large group meeting and asking the leader to try to help the group see the positive aspects of the situation.

A final idea is this: Once all of the ideas have been posted, ask the group to divide itself into small teams to generate ideas to remove the negative aspects from the chart. For an idea to be removed from the chart, the small group must write a specific plan or strategy for its removal. Assign point values to the negative aspects, and award teams points for the aspects they are able to remove from the chart. The team with the most points is declared the winner. This variation puts the responsibility for generating solutions to the problems on the group and gives the members good practice in developing ideas for problem resolution. This practice can pay off down the road as group members tackle more difficult situations.

SOURCE: From *Energizing Staff Meetings* (pp. 79–81), by S. Eller and J. Eller, 2006, Thousand Oaks, CA: Corwin. Copyright 2006 by Corwin. Adapted with permission.

ACTIVITY: COMPARE OUR PERSPECTIVES

Another activity that helps a group to depersonalize conflict is called Compare our Perspectives. This activity involves taking the perspectives in conflict and making them visual. The meeting leader constructs a table that is used to compare the perspectives in a conflict generated by the group. In the table, the general characteristics that will be used to compare the perspectives are written, and the group's task is to complete the table. Once the perspectives are outlined on the table, the group can examine them as data rather than as personal beliefs of group members.

Activity Directions:

• At the time you recognize that opposing perspectives are starting to or presenting the potential to cause a harmful (affective) conflict, stop the conversation, and request that the group engage in the activity Comparing our Perspectives.

• Set up a table or matrix on chart paper on a writing board, as shown in Figure 8.2.

• Engage the group members in identifying their general perceptions of the issue from their view or perspective.

• Once the primary or general or major perspectives have been listed at the top of the chart, ask team members to clarify their comments to ensure that everyone understands the major perspectives on the issue.

• Ask team members to list out specific applications, components, or instances related to the general perspectives listed at the top of the chart. These applications, components, or instances should be clearly related to the general perspectives and written in the columns below each general perspective. These applications, components, or instances can be arranged into themes if they easily fit into themes (as is illustrated in Figure 8.3) or generated and written on the chart randomly.

• Ask team members to talk and compare the general perspectives listed in the top row of the table and the applications, components, or instances listed in the columns. Sometimes, discussions related to perspectives can become emotional and can get out of control. During this conversation you may need to set ground rules or remind group members of their communication norms to keep the conversation on track and productive. Once the conversation has completed, ask the group or team to make decisions about what they want to do in relation to the conflict or varied perceptions of the issues at hand.

Materials/Supplies Needed:

- Chart
- Markers

The immediate purpose of the activity is not to solve the problem but to build a process for people to objectively be able to examine conflict and look at differing perspectives. Once staff members are able to move beyond some of the personal emotion related to conflicts, they will be better able to resolve the natural conflict that occurs in organizations. The process of examining differing perspectives while temporarily withholding their opinions will eventually become part of the school culture. Figure 8.3 provides an example of how a Comparing our Perspectives chart might be completed by a group.

In the example from Figure 8.3, you can see that just listing the components of each perspective does not solve the conflict. The purpose of the activity initially is not to solve the conflict but to provide a visual template that allows the group to begin to deal with the competing issues while removing some of the emotional energy normally associated with the process of working through conflict. When team members verbally advocate for their positions, they have to look at each other. The eye contact and advocacy personalizes the conflict. Team members identify a perspective as "Bill's issue" rather than "an issue." When the components are placed

Figure 8.2 Comparing our Perspectives

Major/Broad Perspective	Perspective 1	Perspective 2	Perspective 3
Component 1			
Component 2			
Component 3			
Component 4			
Component 5			

Figure 8.3 Sample Completed Chart for Comparing our Perspectives

Major/Broad Perspective	Perspective 1 *Teachers are unionized employees on contract and should be paid extra for their time to attend student extracurricular activities.*	Perspective 2 *Teachers are professionals and should be interested in their students. They should attend a few events each year because of their interest in and commitment to the students.*	Perspective 3 *None*
Component 1—Perspectives related to compensation for extra time spent outside of the school day	• Staff members are already expected to give a lot of their time that they are not paid for at the school.	• Part of our job involves supporting our students. We need to be at some of their events.	NA
Component 2—Perspectives related to parent perceptions	• Parents do not understand how much teachers already give to the students.	• We have some flexibility in our schedule because of how the principal works with us.	NA
Component 3—Perspectives related to union rights	• If we give in on this issue, we are turning over one of our union rights, and before you know it, we will be giving away everything.	• Our parent and student population is very supportive of us. We want to keep them on our side.	NA
Component 4—Perspectives related to assessment of student learning and grading	• We are spending too much time correcting student work and planning our lessons to get involved in this type of activity.	• We will gain a lot of good public relations energy from being seen at events. We should go.	NA
Component 5—Perspectives related to student-teacher relationships	• We need to be careful to keep a line or some distance between us and our students.	• Attending events allows us to see the students in a different light and build relationships with them outside of the classroom.	NA

on a matrix, they are looked at for their own value, not as the personal issues of one or more team members.

After staff members become accustomed to looking at the perspective rather than the person or people behind the perspective, conflict takes on a new meaning. Once people internalize the processes of examining and resolving conflict, the culture around resolving conflicts changes.

ACTIVITY: PEELING THE ONION

In many instances, the problems that we face have multiple layers or issues that affect the possible solutions a team can generate. In some of these cases, the problem that is most visible to us is the presenting problem or the symptom of a much deeper issue. It is important that teams be able to peel off the surface issues associated with a problem and get to the core of an issue. In the Peeling the Onion activity, teacher teams get an energizing experience in looking beyond the obvious when working through the problems they may face.

Activity Directions:

• Design a chart like the one shown in Figure 8.4 to help guide the activity.

• Write the most obvious or visible part of the issue in the area that represents the outer part of the onion.

• Ask group members to generate a statement that represents an example of something that is occurring behind the scenes or a factor that could be causing the problem on the outer layer of the onion. The generation of the factor could be done as a large group or through discussions in pairs or other small groups. Writes down the suggestion on the second layer of the onion.

• Now ask the entire group to generate a factor that could be causing the problem or suggestion listed on the second layer of the onion. Write this idea in the third level of the diagram.

• Continue until the group exhausts its ideas.

• Ask the members to talk about what they learned as a result of the activity and to make a decision regarding a solution to the original problem written on the top level of the onion diagram.

Materials/Supplies Needed:

• Peeling the Onion chart
• Markers

Figure 8.4   Peeling the Onion Chart

PEELING THE ONION

Layer 1 Presenting problem

_____

_____

_____

Layer 2 Deeper level affecting the presenting problem

_____

_____

_____

Layer 3 Deeper level affecting Layer 2 situation

_____

_____

_____

Layer 4 Deeper level affecting Layer 3 situation

_____

_____

_____

MEDIATING BETWEEN CONFLICTING PARTIES[1]

As facilitator of a team, you may face situations where people will try to put you in the middle of their disagreements. Consider these strategies to put the ball back in their court and the responsibility back on those involved in the conflict.

- Remain as neutral as possible.
- Let those involved in the conflict know that your role is not to solve their problem; if possible, you would rather not get involved.
- If one of the parties in the conflict approaches you trying to tell his or her side of the story, direct this person back to the source of the conflict.
- When you send a party back to deal with the conflict, be sure to communicate with empathy.
- Avoid carrying information from one party to another.

When you choose to help the parties involved in the conflict work through their issues, consider the following steps.

- Be sure that all parties in conflict are in the room.
- Place yourself somewhere between the conflicting parties, but avoid sitting so that you are not in the direct line of emotional fire.
- Open the conversation by stating your awareness of the problem or situation; then state why you are getting involved and have asked the parties to come together.
- Set the ground rules for the interaction and communication in the meeting (no name calling, listen while the other party is talking, etc.).
- Open the session by asking one of the parties in conflict to state his/her/their perspective while the other party listens. Take notes on what is presented.
- Allow the other person or party to share his/her/their side of the story in regard to the conflict.
- During the time the parties are describing the situation, make no comments that would make it appear that you have taken a side or formed an opinion.
- Summarize what you have heard so far, and ask the parties in conflict to share their perception of what has caused the conflict.

---

1. The following sections are from *Effective Group Facilitation in Education: How to Energize Meetings and Manage Difficult Groups* (pp. 86–89), by J. Eller, 2004, Thousand Oaks, CA: Corwin. Copyright 2004 by Corwin. Reprinted with permission.

- Ask the parties to state what they would like to see happen in order for the conflict to be solved.
- Summarize what you have heard up to this point, and ask participants to agree on a plan to resolve this conflict.
- Help the parties in conflict to develop a follow-up plan. To help it stay on track, discuss possible situations where the plan could run into trouble.
- Summarize the growth you have seen in both parties; thank them for resolving the issue.

During your session, be careful not to get pulled into the conflict, take sides, or solve the problem for the participants. Be sure to find ways to protect yourself from the negative energy that the individuals in conflict will be emitting during this discussion.

PRODUCTIVE INFLUENCE OF CONFLICT ON A TEAM

We have been taught the importance of keeping group meetings smooth and positive. However, it may be good for group members to experience some level of conflict. Here are some of the positive roles of conflict in a group or team:

- Helps a team to define its purpose
- Assists a group in developing team norms or behaviors
- Builds strength or resiliency
- Allows team members to get to know each other and the strengths and weaknesses of the team
- Lets group members experience alternative thoughts and ideas
- Bonds a group together, forms a sense of team

Left unchecked, however, conflict can be damaging to a team. Here are some of the ways that conflict can be damaging to team operations:

- It sets up behavior expectations of team members. (Some members may feel it is their role to cause conflict, others may see themselves as mediators, etc.)
- People on your team may resist coming to meetings in order to avoid conflict
- The focus on conflict may keep team members from accomplishing the tasks the team was assigned.

- Certain members of the group that like conflict may gain power as a result of the constant presence of it on a team.
- A large amount of energy can be used by team members in dealing with conflict.

CONFLICT AND CHAOS

Conflict is closely related to another energy source found in teams called *chaos*. In chaos, the team members have lost some of their control over certain aspects of their operation. Dr. Margaret Wheatley, in her book *Leadership and the New Science* (1999), calls chaos a positive force that helps us to redefine ourselves. She also states that most groups have to experience some form of chaos in order to come out of a situation better than when they went into it. Here are some forms of chaos that groups may experience.

- Unclear expectations
- Changing direction
- Reduced budgets for implementation of their decision
- Changing leadership
- Unclear procedures for team operation
- Disagreement among team members
- Attempts to manage problems outside the group's control
- Disruptions caused by others outside the group

Chaos is one of the stages that M. S. Peck, in his book, *The Different Drum* (1998), has identified as a part of the process of a group developing into a community. While chaos is important to a group, there are some ideas to keep in mind in relation to chaos and the development of community. They are as follows:

- Understand that chaos is a natural force that most groups and organizations go through in order to form a group or community. Small doses of chaos can be good for a team, while large doses can cause trouble.
- While it might be tempting to introduce chaos to a group, be careful with this strategy. There is probably enough chaos occurring naturally to provide a team the opportunity to work through it.
- You will notice that as teams are experiencing chaos, members will want to quickly move out of it. They may ask you to provide answers to their problems instead of working through them on their own. Don't rescue them right away.
- While a group you are working with is experiencing chaos, you may not feel that you are doing a good job with them. Resist this feeling, and know that by letting the group work through the chaos, you are helping them work toward community.

SUMMARY

Helping a group work through conflict is an important part of improving the climate of a school. Understanding that conflict is a normal part of people working together is a first step toward making productive use of the energy normally associated with conflict. In this chapter, we have provided you with a variety of activities to help your group work through conflict and find ways to work together as a team.

9

*Celebrating
Your Success*

It's been written in many books and said by many experts in the field for a number of years that what is important in an organization is what gets the attention. We can tell people that we really appreciate their contributions, but unless we celebrate and recognize those contributions, the people don't really know that we appreciate them. In many projects, we plan to look at the deficits of the organization and then consider what needs to be put into place for the group to be successful and the strategic planning that needs to go into the project. But we normally forget a very important part—to plan a celebration once we are successful.

ABOUT THIS CHAPTER

In this chapter, you will learn the following:

- The importance of planning up front for a celebration based on the success of the project
- The role of celebrations and rituals in the improvement of school climate and culture
- Ideas and strategies to plan celebrations, from the simple and straightforward to the more complex

Many of use work in organizations made up of people who are constantly on the go. We are always working on the next "thing" and not always paying attention to the human elements and details that are crucial to the success of our schools and districts. Although this frenzy seems normal, people will notice when you focus on celebrating the small successes. Let's see how Charlie, the principal of Focus High School, uses celebrations to thank people for their hard work and build a supportive and functional culture:

> Charlie, the principal of Focus High School, holds regular celebrations to reward and thank staff members for their hard work and dedication. At the first meeting of each planning group or task force at the school, he requires that staff members think about what they will do to celebrate once the project is successful. He has found that the success rate and visibility of his projects have increased since he started requiring celebration planning at the start of the project. He also holds a monthly celebration meeting with staff members to recognize the contributions individuals have made to the success of the school. The awards furnished by Charlie's parent organization are small but coveted by teachers. He asks his shop teacher to have students in the industrial technology classes make the trophies and plaques he passes out to the staff. It is not the actual plaque or trophy that motivates the teachers but the thought that someone actually appreciated what they did that makes the difference. Charlie has positively impacted the staff culture as a result of his efforts to celebrate the small successes on his staff.

As you can see from this example, celebrations hold an important function in the shaping of school climate and culture. In this chapter we will look at strategies you can use to improve the climate and culture of your school through the use of celebrations and thanking people for their efforts.

STRATEGY: PLANNING THE CELEBRATION AT THE START OF THE INITIATIVE

In schools we do a lot of planning. We have strategic plans, long-range plans, short-term plans, budget plans, and so forth. We don't always do a good job in planning how we will celebrate and recognize success. In our own experiences and in the experiences of other successful administrators, planning for a celebration at the start of an initiative is crucial. In many cases, we have used the planning process to identify what the successfully completed project will look like and the exact activities that we will do to celebrate our success. In Figure 9.1 there is an example of how we integrated planning for success into a normal planning process.

PLANNING FOR SUCCESS AND CELEBRATION

General Office Goal: _____

Project Area of Focus: _____

Team Members Working on Project: _____

1. General Goal Statement	2. Present Level of Functioning	3. Gap Between Present Level of Achievement and Desired Level of Achievement	4. Strategies Needed to Be Successful With Goal Area	5. Timeline for Implementation	6. People Responsible for Strategies or Goal Area	7. Vision of What School Will Look Like if the Goal Is Attained

Celebration Planning

Vision of successful project completion (from column 7 above)

Specific plans for celebration _____

Date/time/location for celebration _____

SOURCE: From *Effective Group Facilitation in Education: How to Energize Meetings and Manage Difficult Groups*, by J. Eller, 2004, Thousand Oaks, CA: Corwin. Copyright 2004 by Corwin. Reprinted with permission.

135

ACTIVITY: HIGH FIVES

Celebrations do not have to be complex in nature in order to positively impact the climate and culture of a school. This simple but effective technique works well.

Activity Directions:

• Call the staff together for a short meeting some time during the school day.

• Have everyone attending the meeting stand together in a huddle.

• Announce the success of the project and share your feelings about the project.

• Ask staff members to give each other "high fives" in celebration of the event.

The staff members leave the meeting charged and energized.

Materials/Supplies Needed:

• None

ACTIVITY: BANANA SPLITS

Food can be an effective motivator for staff and can be used effectively for celebrations. This strategy can be both motivating and mysterious at the same time.

Activity Directions:

• Place a banana in each staff member's mailbox. Attach a note using the language listed below:

"Bring this banana and your appetite to a staff meeting at 3:30 p.m. today. We will be talking about our recent success in raising student achievement."

• When staff members show up at the meeting, greet them with several tubs of ice cream, bowls, and various toppings.

• Tell staff members they may make sundaes; as they make the sundaes, talk about the success of the program and the reason for the celebration.

• Suggest that staff members share their own thoughts about the success, thank each other, and mingle during the eating time.

Materials/Supplies Needed:

- A banana for each staff member
- Ice cream and toppings
- Bowls, spoons, and napkins

SOURCE: Rick Whipler, Stillwater Junior High School.

ACTIVITY: GALLERY WALK

Visual touchstones or reminders really help people connect to a successful event. The experience becomes much more meaningful when they can actually "see" it for themselves. Here is an example of how this strategy can be implemented.

Activity Directions:

- Gather up artifacts related to the area of success.

- Enlarge photocopies of these artifacts, or list them on chart paper.

- Place the enlarged artifacts or charts on the walls of the room where a staff meeting will be held.

- When staff members come into the room, talk about the success of the project and why it was successful.

- Divide the staff members into smaller teams of two to three people.

- Give the teams time to walk around the room examining the artifacts or charts and holding discussions related to the success of the project. As teams are engaging in this gallery walk, play motivational music lightly in the background.

- Once all of the artifacts or charts have been examined, have the entire group talk about the success of the project.

Materials/Supplies Needed:

- Enlarged photocopies of artifacts or prepared lists of artifacts
- Recordings of motivational music and appropriate music player

STRATEGY: TROPHY CASE DISPLAYS

Schools routinely use trophy cases to display the products of success from athletic and extracurricular events. Trophy cases can also be used to display the products of success from other endeavors as well. We have seen schools display letters of commendation from state officials, their most recent graduation information, aggregated test scores that show successes, awards or grants, positive newspaper articles about the school, and so forth in a prominent trophy case at the school. If you use this strategy, make sure the trophy case is in an area that will attract attention, displays the accomplishment appropriately, and draws attention to the positive aspect of the accomplishment.

STRATEGY: GET OUT OF DUTY CARDS

Teachers are busy throughout the day, and sometimes the thought of doing another duty can be overwhelming. One strategy we have used as a reward/celebration opportunity is the Get Out of Duty card. The card is based on the Get Out of Jail Free card in a Monopoly game, and it provides a great visual for teachers to see that their efforts on a project were appreciated. Here is how it works:

- Upon hearing of the accomplishment or success, visit the classrooms of the teachers involved in the successful project.

- While visiting the classrooms, issue a Get Out of Duty card to each teacher involved in the success of the project.

- When the teacher wants to redeem the card, cover a duty for the teacher.

- The coverage of a duty normally has some stipulations:
  - The card must be turned in one day before the duty is scheduled.
  - The duty must be scheduled for a time at which you are free to cover it.
  - Cards may not be turned in during the last two weeks of the school year.

STRATEGY: SUCCESS THERMOMETER

We all understand the importance of visuals and visualizing in schools. When people have a clear view of the success of a project, it is more likely to be successful. Many fundraising agencies in the community display a large thermometer in a central location in a town where a community drive or fundraising event is being held. As money is being raised, the "fluid" in the thermometer rises. This provides a clear view of the pathway for success for the community.

Schools have used this concept successfully. Here are some of the examples we have seen:

- A large thermometer was placed in the central entrance of a high school. It listed the percentages of students that had passed the graduation test. The staff gathered around it and celebrated when the school reached its target goal.

- At another school, a line drawing of the school was placed in the center hallway. The school improvement goals were listed at the bottom of the drawing. As the school accomplished its goals, color was added to the drawing using markers. Staff members and students gathered around the drawing periodically to gauge the progress of the project. When the project was completed, a celebration was held by the drawing. The drawing helped people to emotionally connect with the project and its success.

- A success meter was placed on a school's Web site and on the screen saver page for school computers. As the project unfolded, the meter was updated to reflect the progress toward the goal. The staff started to really get excited as the meter filled in. Once it was full (the project was completed successfully), a celebration was held. Enlarged printed pictures of the completed meter were used as table centerpieces during the celebration at a staff meeting.

SUMMARY

Humans are driven by emotions and positive experiences. In order to improve the climate of your school, you need to find ways to overtly recognize and celebrate the success of your projects and initiatives. In this chapter, you have been provided with ideas and strategies to help you as you use this positive tool in motivating your staff members.

In Chapter 10, Supporting Climate and Culture Change as a Leader, you will learn ideas to move your change efforts forward in a successful manner. You will also learn subtle but powerful ways to support your staff as the climate and culture of your school begin to improve. Be staying focused and using small, integrated strategies, you will be successful in your efforts to improve the climate and ultimately the culture of your school.

10

Supporting Climate and Culture Change as a Leader

As the principal of a school, you are responsible to assess the climate and culture and then support the staff in moving forward to positively change these crucial aspects. There are many ideas and strategies you can employ to provide the structure and support needed for improvement to occur. We have shared many of these with you in the previous chapters of this book. This last chapter is devoted to specific behaviors of school principals that we have found to be helpful in moving the school climate and ultimately the culture in a positive direction. Many of the ideas you will read about may seem like they are based on common sense, and everyone should know how to use them in a school. Surprisingly, we have worked with principals who have never had the support, mentoring, and staff development opportunities to learn these ideas.

Here's an example from a principal we know who recently became the leader of a middle school that had a history of a difficult climate and culture. She was able to turn the school around.

Helen, the new principal of Terrace Middle School, had her work cut out for her. The school she was chosen to lead had a reputation for very poor staff member relations. Helen knew that in order for the student learning environment to be productive, the adult working environment had to be professional and productive. In a meeting with the staff at the start of the school year, she asked people to divide into small groups to develop a list of their expectations of her as the leader. At the same time, Helen was developing her own list of expectations for the staff. After about 45 minutes, she asked small groups to share their expectations. She shared her expectations with the group.

As the year progressed, she noticed that relationships among the staff were operating mostly in an open and positive manner. Helen made it a priority to spend time in classrooms, walk around the school, connect with custodians and cooks, and interact with her office staff to assess how people were treating each other.

In mid-October, Helen picked up some information about an emerging conflict between a custodian and a teaching team. She met individually with each of the parties and quickly assessed that she needed to meet with the team and the custodian together to mediate the tension and get things back on track. At the meeting, Helen laid out the ground rules for the session and then allowed the teachers and the custodian to share their perspectives on the situation. Helen managed the behaviors of the fighting factions in order to reinforce the expectations that were set in the first meeting of the fall. In the end, the team and the custodian that were in conflict were able to get their behaviors on track. They also learned something; Helen had drawn a line in the sand that no one would be allowed to cross. This line helped staff members to figure out how communication would be handled in the new culture that was emerging at the school.

In the example shared here, Helen took it upon herself to follow through, insisting that staff meet the new expectations for staff behavior, communication, and relationships at her school. She had previously worked through and developed these expectations with the staff, but now, through taking the bull by the horns, she was actually teaching them that she expected them to meet the expectations. She was modeling and teaching the staff how to follow through themselves on the agreed-upon climate and culture initiatives.

ABOUT THIS CHAPTER

In this chapter, we will present ideas to help you as you work to improve the climate and culture of your school. As you read the chapter, look for the following:

- Subtle and natural strategies that you can integrate into your daily routines to improve the climate and culture of your school

- The steps that you need to have in place in order to successfully implement and track your school improvement project
- Natural pitfalls or roadblocks you may encounter as you implement your project (resistance, implementation blockers)

As you work to improve the climate and culture of the school, remember that not everyone wants to see the project be successful. In any culture, there are people who have been benefiting from the status quo of the school. Sometimes a dysfunctional school culture allows people to hide, and in other cases, it keeps them from becoming totally accountable for their actions.

In our book, *Energizing Staff Meetings* (Eller & Eller, 2006), we provided a set of steps that principals can use when implementing new ideas or changes. These steps also are important to keep in mind as you move forward on school climate and culture changes:

- Understand your strengths, weaknesses, and inhibitions.
- Build a seedbed.
- Plant the seeds.
- Nurture them; watch them grow.
- Pull the weeds.
- Harvest the crop.

A brief explanation of each of these components is listed below.

STEP 1: UNDERSTAND YOUR STRENGTHS, WEAKNESSES, AND INHIBITIONS[1]

As the leader of school climate and culture improvement initiatives, assess your strengths, weaknesses, and inhibitions related to the improvement effort. Here are some strategies to consider:

- List all of the steps that need to be implemented in order for the change effort to be successful; examine how you stack up to those needs.
- Think about which parts of the project are comfortable for you and which parts are uncomfortable for you. Decide how you will overcome your inhibitions.
- Think about the amount of time required for, the potential impact of, and the organizational strife that may be caused by this initiative. Decide whether the cost is worth the gain.

---

1. Steps 1–6 are from *Energizing Staff Meetings* (pp. 161–169), by S. Eller and J. Eller, 2006, Thousand Oaks, CA: Corwin. Copyright 2006 by Corwin. Adapted with permission.

STEP 2: BUILD A SEEDBED

A successful school climate project is like a garden; they both need a strong seedbed to be successful. Here are some strategies to help you nurture the seedbed:

- Talk with key staff members about the need to improve the climate and culture of the school.
- Form a committee to study ways to impact the climate.
- Bring up the idea of improving the climate and culture of the school at a faculty meeting; allow people a chance to talk about the pros and cons of an initiative.
- Provide teachers with articles about the importance of school climate and culture; hold discussion groups on the topic.
- Provide copies of this book to key staff members so that they can read about and understand the importance of an improved climate and culture.

STEP 3: PLANT THE SEEDS

As you sense that a foundation is forming for the success of your project, begin initial implementation. When you start with small efforts, you are *planting the seeds* for success. These initial project trials will give you important information that you can use when you get ready to implement ideas across the entire school. Here are some strategies that other principals have used:

- A principal worked with two teachers to help them learn about climate and culture. The teachers took some of the ideas and implemented them in their classrooms. They brought what they had learned to share at a staff meeting.
- At a high school, a principal worked with the department chairs to teach them how to improve the climate of their department meetings. They met on a monthly basis to share what they were learning and how it might help the entire school improve the working climate for the staff.
- A principal launched a climate and culture improvement effort by bringing in an outside consultant. The consultant shared some ideas with the staff, asked them to share some of the school's climate and culture issues at the training session, and helped the principal and staff to formulate several initial goals for the improvement of these elements in the school. Later the consultant followed up on how the staff was doing in relation to the two or three ideas they were implementing.

STEP 4: NURTURE THEM; WATCH THEM GROW

Just like a young plant, projects need nurturing to help them survive and grow. Here are several strategies we have seen successfully used in improving school climate and culture:

- The principal thanks the staff for their participation in the climate and culture improvement project.
- The leader points out the growth that he or she has seen in the staff as a result of the improvement efforts.
- Staff members coach each other to continue the growth they have seen as a result of the climate and culture initiative.
- The group leader provides extra release time as a reward for the work that the planning team has done to implement the climate and culture improvement project.
- The project is broken into parts, and periodic celebrations are scheduled and conducted to reinforce the efforts of staff members.

STEP 5: PULL THE WEEDS

As the project unfolds, problems may arise. Like weeds in a garden, problems left unchecked will kill the project. Try the following strategies when you sense problems are arising:

- Deal with implementation blockers.
- Monitor the school, including classrooms and the teachers' lounge. When you hear negative comments that indicate backsliding is occurring, ask staff members to clarify their positions.
- As the projects unfold, be on the lookout for individuals who seem not to be using agreed-upon actions or behaviors. Sit down with these individuals, and talk through the concerns they have with the project.
- Look for slippage or backsliding, where people move back to their old behaviors. Review the expectations again, and follow up to make sure people are implementing the ideas they agreed upon.

Negative Staff Members Who Undermine
Your Efforts (Implementation Blockers)

Implementation blockers is a term that we use to describe people on the staff who like the idea that things never change. These people may benefit in some manner from the status quo. They will work behind the scenes to undermine some very well-intended efforts by you and other staff members to move the group forward. There are some key behaviors that can tip you off that you have an implementation blocker on your hands:

- Eye rolling during meetings at which climate and culture activities or strategies are implemented
- Laughing or snickering when climate improvement strategies are introduced
- Meeting in small groups before a meeting; these small groups stop talking when you come near them
- Hesitating to move when directed to change groups or activities during the meeting
- Undermining of discussions at culture and climate improvement meetings by one or two individuals acting as spokespersons for a disaffected subgroup

Some of these comments could include the following:

"Many of us on the faculty feel that these activities are a waste of time."

"I spoke to the parent group and they agree with our concerns."

"All of the staff members I have spoken to have some concerns about this new effort."

Implementation blockers will try to get you to abandon your improvement efforts by undermining your confidence in your leadership and in the meeting strategies you are implementing. Here is a way to deal with their comments:

- Listen to the message, ask clarifying questions, and seek to understand the origin of the concern. Normally, implementation blockers cannot back up their assertions when pressed for specificity.
- Listen to the core of their comments to see whether their concerns have any merit. Address those concerns right away.
- Listen to the language that implementation blockers use; analyze it for specificity. Normally, they will be very vague or general in their description of their concern.
- Be ready to share the big picture and the supporting details of your efforts. Even if you don't think that they will agree with you or believe you, share your overall plan. If you are specific, it can take some of the bite out of their arguments.
- Agree to check in with them at a future date to see whether they still have concerns.

STEP 6: HARVEST THE CROP

Finally, if you are successful with the improvement effort, you will be able to harvest the reward and see the fruits of your labor.

SUMMARY

Even though school climate and culture can be complex issues, they can also be influenced through careful thought and planning. In this chapter we have discussed the major ideas you need to keep in mind as you move forward with your efforts to improve the climate and culture of your school. Good luck as you work to implement your efforts; your hard work will be worth it in the end when the functioning and problem-solving capacities of your school have improved and the climate and culture are in place to help children grow and succeed.

References

Dickmann, M., Stanford-Blair, N., & Rosati-Bojar, A. (2004). *Leading with the brain in mind: 101 brain compatible practices for leaders.* Thousand Oaks, CA: Corwin.

Eller, J. (2004). *Effective group facilitation in education: How to energize meetings and manage difficult groups.* Thousand Oaks, CA: Corwin.

Eller, J., & Carlson, H. (2008) *So, now you're the superintendent.* Thousand Oaks, CA: Corwin.

Eller, S., & Eller J. (2006). *Energizing staff meetings.* Thousand Oaks, CA: Corwin.

Hoy, A., & Hoy, W. (2009). *Instructional leadership: A research-based guide to learning in schools.* Boston: Pearson.

Hoyle, J. (1982). *Guidelines for the preparation of school administrators.* Arlington, VA: American Association of School Administrators.

Kochanek, J. (2005). *Building trust for better schools.* Thousand Oaks, CA: Corwin.

Kouzes, J., & Posner, B., (2007). *The leadership challenge.* San Francisco: Jossey-Bass.

Newstrom, J. W., & Scannell, E. (1998). *The big book of team-building games: Trust-building activities, team spirit exercises, and other fun things to do.* New York: McGraw-Hill.

Peck, M. S. (1998). *The different drum: Community making and peace.* New York: Touchstone.

Schein, E. (2004). *Organizational culture and leadership.* San Francisco: Jossey-Bass.

Sergiovanni, T. (2007). *Rethinking leadership: A collection of articles* (2nd ed.) Thousand Oaks, CA: Corwin.

Wheatley, M. (1995). *Leadership and the new science: Discovering order in a chaotic world.* San Francisco: Berrett-Koehler.

Index